A Sequential Sojourn:

Visualizing the Quest of

the Archetypal Hero

Susan R. Woodward

To My Guides: *Thalia, Mimi, and Candy*

To My Companions: *Illy and Mark, Jim, Robin and Sean,*
Sarah and Dietrich, Joe, and Jordan

To My Heroes Whose Journey Ended Far Too Soon:
Dolores Franklin
Barbara L. Stanfield
James L. Woodward
May our paths cross again on the other side.

Welcome to Sharing in the Quest of the Archetypal Hero!

I am happy to share with you *A Sequential Sojourn* toward your personal goals and dreams. The quest of the hero permeates not only our culture, but all cultures across time and geographic location. This quest is part of the human condition and can be used as a tool to examine our own lives. We are the heroes of our own life stories; how those stories ultimately play out will be based on our reactions to life's challenges and the decisions we make.

Through visualization, the guided meditations will take you on a journey through your imagination. While the basics of each meditation are set for you, each person will create his her own experience through the specifics you will be asked to provide. An area for writing down the specific things you encounter or experience is provided at the end of each session. From there introspection questions are provided for you to use as a guide for writing about your own journey.

In exploring our own life patterns, it will help us to see that we are all connected through our stories and experiences. We all have goals, trials to face, dragons to slay, and our reward awaits us for a job well done!

These two are obviously different, yet they manage to share living space. I wonder what THEY talk about! May we who are different also find our commonalities!

The *Sequential Sojourn* is an effort to draw people of various nations, cultures, ages, and genders together to examine the things that make us similar. So much effort is spent on diversity (which is a good thing, don't get me wrong) that we are more conscious of how we are different from one another than of how we are alike.

With a bit of tolerance, perhaps finding the hero within can help create positive change in this troubled world.

Cultural Mythology and Societal Beliefs

All cultures have stories that try to explain the unexplainable. That is one thing that humanity has is common. The important thing to remember is that it is not so much a question of WHAT people believe as it is one of WHY they believe it. Beliefs surrounding creation (making sense of the past), social/moral duty (the present), and death (the future) are what all cultures across time and geographic location have in common. When the "what" becomes more important than the "why", conflicts of disastrous proportions arise ("MY beliefs are better than YOUR beliefs"). By examining human history, it is easy to find many examples of how a group of people were cruel to other groups based on the stories they believe to be true (religious intolerance). If people realized that the basis for these stories arise from man's need to know about the unexplainable, then perhaps greater tolerance could prevail.

Stories in every culture are created to explain:

The Past:

- creation myths
- birth of hcrocs/gods/goddcsscs
- answers to a child's questions
  - What is thunder? (How many of you were told that it is the angels bowling?)
  - Where do babies come from? (Common stories include the cabbage patch or a stork.)
- responses from adults to the child's queries vary:
  - "Why do you want to know?" (stalling to come up with an answer)
  - "I don't know" (the most honest answer)
  - "Just because" or "Because I said so" (frustration from not knowing the answer)

- making up a story (alleviates the frustration for both parent and child)
- telling an age-old story (passes on the beliefs of the culture)

The Present:

- CREDO of a culture (the values/beliefs of the society) is known to those who live in that society.
- Heroes arise who exemplify those values and beliefs (usually based on factual people and/or events that have been blown out of proportion through retelling, much like the telephone game)

The Future:

- What happens after death? This is one of man's greatest fears, and so these stories told were to create a sense of comfort.
- Some leaders use fear of the unknown as a manipulative tool in order to maintain a sense of order in society.
  - good/bad
  - reward/punishment
  - if.....then...

Recurring Motifs

Besides being asked to contemplate on the hero's quest itself, within the visualizations, you will be asked to pay attention to certain motifs or symbols that may recur. For example, in many cases, the archetypal hero is called to begin his adventure in the spring. Spring symbolizes new beginnings when the plants begin to bud, and the Earth is renewed. As the story progresses, the hero's main tests and trials usually occur in the autumn, a time of change.

The following is a chart of familiar motifs that are present throughout myths and legends around the world. For each direction on the wheel, I have listed:

- a season associated with the direction (For example, east may be associated with spring because both represent new beginnings. The sun rises in the east just as new plants bud in spring.)
- a natural element so that the reader may pay attention to animals, birds, or other creatures that may be associated with that element (For example, many Native American tribes associate East with the element air. All creatures of the air, therefore, can be associated with this direction.)
- colors that can symbolize the archetypal hero's progress on his/her journey (For example, it is common for the hero to wear green, which is associated with growth.)
- a goal that the hero is seeking by going that that particular direction which may be associated with the natural element (For example, going east may be considered a quest for knowledge, since many cultures associate that direction with knowledge or thoughts.)
- how that goal may be associated with the hero's level of progress on his/her quest (For example, since East represents new beginnings, then the hero's quest will still be in the idea or thinking stage.)
- questions that can associate with the archetypal hero's progress

Cycle of Growth

North

- Winter
- Earth
- brown, black, white
- material world
- manifestation of ideas
- What does the hero accomplish? (death of former self)

West

- Autumn
- water (fluidity)
- blue, purple
- emotions
- benefits to self/others
- How has the hero changed?

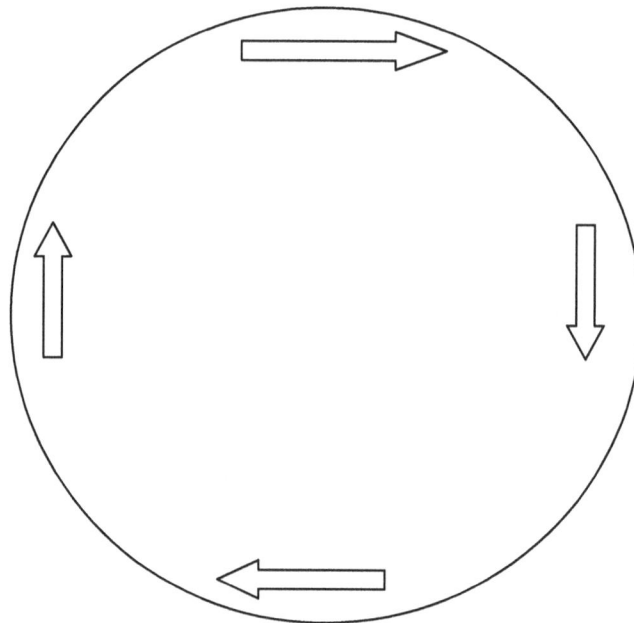

East

- Spring
- air
- green, yellow
- knowledge
- ideas
- What does the hero need to learn?

South

- Summer
- fire
- red, orange
- creativity
- planning
- How is the hero growing?

Outlining the Sequential Sojourn

Day 1: A Hero Lies In You

How do you define a hero? Please share what qualities you believe make someone "heroic" and give examples of heroes you have encountered throughout your life.

Read the lyrics to the following song that was performed by Mariah Carey. While reading, think about what qualities you already possess that you could use to make a difference in the world. A hero does lie within you; how can you bring him/her to the surface?

"Hero"
by Mariah Carey and Walter Afanasieff

There's a hero if you look inside your heart
You don't have to be afraid of what you are
There's an answer if you reach into your soul
And the sorrow that you know will melt away

And then a hero comes along
With the strength to carry on
And you cast your fears aside
And you know you can survive
So when you feel like hope is gone
Look inside you and be strong
And you'll finally see the truth
That a hero lies in you

It's a long road when you face the world alone
No one reaches out a hand for you to hold
You can find love if you search within yourself

And the emptiness you felt will disappear

And then a hero comes along
With the strength to carry on
And you cast your fears aside
And you know you can survive
So when you feel like hope is gone
Look inside you and be strong
And you'll finally see the truth
That a hero lies in you

Lord knows dreams are hard to follow
But don't let anyone tear them away
Hold on
There will be tomorrow
In time you'll find the way

Your Reaction:

_____

_____

_____

_____

_____

_____

Identifying your Heroic Archetype

Stories about heroes are part of every culture across time and geographic location. Joseph Campbell, in *The Hero with a Thousand Faces,* identified both the archetype of the Hero and the Journey that the hero follows, and demonstrated how that pattern is woven throughout the myths and legends of the world. Carol Pearson, in *Awakening The Heroes Within* expands upon Campbell's idea of the Hero into twelve distinct archetypes, each of which can follow the Hero's Journey.

What follows is a brief description of each of Pearson's twelve archetypes. After reading through theses descriptions, select the one that you seem to most identify with and explain why this archetype best fits who you are at this time.

Innocent

The Innocent, fearing abandonment, seeks safety. The Innocent's greatest strength is the trust and optimism that endears him/her to others, so he/she is able to gain help and support on his/her quest. The Innocent's main danger is that he/she may be blind to his/her obvious weaknesses or perhaps deny them. He/She can also become dependent on others to fulfill his/her heroic tasks.

Orphan

The Orphan, fearing exploitation, seeks to regain the comfort of the womb and neonatal safety in the arms of loving parents. To fulfill his/her quest, he/she must go through the agonies of the developmental stages he/she have missed. The Orphan's strength is the interdependence and pragmatic realism that he/she had to learn at an early age. A hazard is that he/she will fall into the victim mentality and so never achieve a heroic position.

Warrior

The Warrior is relatively simple in his/her thought patterns, seeking simply to win whatever confronts him/her, including the dragons that live inside the mind and his/her underlying fear of weakness. The Warrior's challenge is to bring meaning to what he/she does; perhaps choosing his/her battles wisely, which is done using courage and the warrior's discipline.

Caregiver

Caregivers first seek to help others, which they do with compassion and generosity. A risk they take is that in their pursuit to help others they may end up being harmed themselves. They dislike selfishness, especially in themselves, and fear what it might make them.

Seeker

The Seeker is looking for something that will improve his/her life in some way, but in doing so may not realize that he/she have much already inside the self. The Seeker embraces learning and is ambitious in his/her quest and often avoids the encumbrance of support from others. Needing to 'do it themselves', Seekers keep moving until they find their goal (and usually their true self too).

Lover

The Lover seeks the bliss of true love and the syzygy (cosmic union) of the divine couple. The Lover often shows the passion that he/she seeks in a relationship in his/her energy and commitment to gaining the reciprocal love of another. Lovers fear both being alone and losing the love that they have gained, driving them to constantly sustain their love relationships.

Destroyer

The Destroyer is a paradoxical character whose destructiveness reflects the death drive and an inner fear of annihilation. As a fighter, he/she is thus careless of his/her own safety and may put others in danger, too. The

Destroyer's quest is to change, to let go of his/her anger or whatever force drives him/her and return to balance, finding the life drive that will sustain him/her. Living on the cusp of life and death, the Destroyer is often surprisingly humble.

Creator

Creators, fearing that all is an illusion, seek to prove reality outside of their minds.

A critical part of their quest is in finding and accepting themselves, discovering their true identity in relation to the external world.

Ruler

The Ruler's quest is to create order and structure and hence an effective society in which the subjects of the Ruler can live productive and relatively happy lives. This is not necessarily an easy task, as order and chaos are not far apart, and the Ruler has to commit himself (or herself) fully to the task. The buck stops with him/her, and he/she must thus be wholly responsible -- for which the Ruler needs ultimate authority.

Magician

The Magician's quest is not to 'do magic' but to transform or change something or someone in some way. The Magician has significant power and as such may be feared. Magicians may also fear themselves and their potential to do harm. Perhaps their ultimate goal is to transform themselves, achieving a higher plane of existence.

Sage

The Sage is a seeker after truth and enlightenment and journeys far in search of the next golden nugget of knowledge. The danger for the Sage and his/her deep fear is that his/her hard-won wisdom is built on the sand of falsehood.

The Sage's best hope is that he/she plays from a position of objective honesty and learns to see with a clarity that knows truth and untruth.

Fool

The goal of the Fool is perhaps the wisest goal of all, which is just to enjoy life as it is, with all its paradoxes and dilemmas. What causes most dread in the Fool is a lack of stimulation and being 'not alive'. Fools must seek to 'be', perhaps as the Sage, but may not understand this.

Your Heroic Archetype:

_____

_____

_____

_____

_____

Day 2: A World Without Heroes

Before we begin discussing how the journey of the hero permeates not only world cultures but our very lives, one thing we might want to think about is what the world might be like if there were no heroes.

The rock group KISS produced a thought-provoking song that addresses this topic.

What are your thoughts about what the world might be like if no one ever stood up to make a difference?

"A World Without Heroes"
by Paul Stanley, Bob Ezrin, Lou Reed, Gene Simmons
as performed by KISS

A world without heroes
Is like a world without sun
You can't look up to anyone
Without heroes
And a world without heroes
Is like a never ending race
Is like a time without a place
A pointless thing devoid of grace

Well you don't know what you're after
Or if something's after you
And you don't know why you don't know
In a world without heroes

In a world without dreams
Things are no more than they seem
And a world without heroes

Is like a bird without wings

Or a bell that never rings

Such a sad and useless thing

Where you don't know what you're after

Or if something's after you

Well you don't know why you don't know

And a world without heroes

Is nothing to be

It's no place for me.

What would a world without heroes be like?

_____

_____

_____

_____

_____

_____

Day 3: *Beau Fleuve*

by Susan R. Woodward

Drip, drip,

Drip, drip;

An icicle tip

Feeds a tiny spring below.

Drip, drip,

Drip, drip;

Carried away

By the water's gentle flow,

Effortlessly gliding

Around objects to and fro;

A rock here,

A stump there,

Form a meandering path

Winding its way

In search of a sister--

Separate tributaries fallen from the same tree;

Mere capillaries in the stream of life.

Two finally meet

And then another

And another.

With strength in numbers they carry forth

Babbling together as they travel.

Having no need for detours,

Rocks and stumps are hurdled over;

Each triumph is greeted with gurgles and splashes of laughter.

Love is nurtured and they flow like veins toward a common goal.

Further along, other families fall in.

Members mingle in a roar of introductions as everyone tries to talk at once;

Not until all are on even ground does the din dim.

Still more join in the journey from far-away places and their numbers swelled--

One river born from many streams,

Rolled in one blaze of blinding light.

Awed into silence, a higher power calls each to unite and follow;

None can ignore the call of the Current.

The love pulsating surges through every one;

They pick up the beat and flow forward drawing strength from one another

Until each comes to his destined course and is sent outward on his mission.

The river branches and reaches toward the surrounding land

Like oxygen-fed arteries carrying rich nourishment.

Life is sustained along the path as

Creatures of the forest

And photosynthesized friends are fed.

The outreach continues

With splintered streams

That eventually whittle down to

Trickling trails of life

Seeping into the ground.

Mettle is tested below the surface

With blind floundering

Hoping to be led toward Spring.

At last! Spring is found

And again emerges from the depths

To greet the newcomers from above;

Drip, drip,

Drip, drip,

Drip, drip.

After reading the poem "Beau Fleuve", what images or allusions can you find that relate to the cyclical patterns of life?

What do you notice about the shape of the poem?

How can this poem relate to the journey of the archetypal hero?

Day 4: The Whisper From Within

Find a comfortable position in a quiet place where you will not be disturbed. Read the meditation slowly and carefully. Be sure to pause to allow for visualization.

Close your eyes and relax. Now take three deep breaths: one for body, one for mind, and one for spirit. Take one last very deep breath and hold it. Just when you think you cannot hold the breath any longer, pull in just a bit more air. Again, when you feel as if you cannot continue holding the breath, pull in just a little more. When you finally do release your breath, do so very slowly in a long continuous exhale until you have released all that you were holding. Breathe slowly and deeply as you continue to relax. Relax all the muscles of your body: your legs, your arms, your shoulders, and your jaw. Completely relax.

Imagine that you are sinking down into the furniture, and in turn sinking through the floor. Allow yourself to continue sinking down and down, all the while feeling completely relaxed. You pass deep down into the earth and suddenly find yourself in a vast cave, nestled comfortably in the bottom of a shallow boat. There are soft blankets around you, keeping you warm and relaxed. The boat is caught by the current of a narrow river, and you find yourself floating along, emerging from the darkness of the cave. The river flows through a lush green forest, and the sky above is a deep blue. You are able to lie back, looking up at the trees as the boat continues to float through the forest. As you float along, the tree branches overhead become more intertwined, and the boat enters what seems to be a tunnel through the trees. Even though the sun is now only filtering through the trees, you still feel relaxed and centered as the boat continues on its course. The sound of birdsong lulls you into a deeper state of relaxation, and you watch the gentle breeze rippling the leaves above you.

After a while, the boat gently comes to a stop at a sandy bank. You are now deep in the forest, and the birdsong has begun to dissipate. The only sound at the moment is the gentle rustling of the breeze.

Getting out of the boat, you find yourself near a very large, very old tree. Taking a deep breath, the scent of the forest is familiar to you, and you feel as if you've been here before. It's a pleasant feeling, even though you cannot remember precisely when you'd been here.

The breeze picks up slightly, but with it comes a new sound. At first you think you are hearing things, but as the sound comes again, you cannot deny what you hear. It is the sound of someone calling your name. It comes again, yet you are not afraid. It almost seems natural to hear your name being spoken in this place. Listen to the voice calling you. What is the pitch of the voice? Is it a high or a low pitch? What about the tone? Does it seem imploring? Demanding? Beaconing?

You search for the source of the calling, and after walking around the area, you realize that the sound is coming from within the large, old tree. Seeing a hole in the tree, you realize that it must be hollow, and the voice echoes from within. You are not afraid, but mesmerized by the sound, and you come closer to the tree. Peeking into the hole, you see something glinting just inside. Reaching in, you find a beautiful hand mirror just inside the hole, and the voice becomes louder and more insistent. It's coming from the mirror itself.

You look into the mirror and are surprised at your reflection. You do not see what you expect, which is the face you've come to know since birth. What you see is something deeper inside, though still recognizable as you; it is the heroic archetype you have selected for yourself.

Gazing into your own eyes, what do you find there? The mirror image speaks nothing more than your name, yet the expression on his/her face speaks volumes. Memorize the image in the mirror and gauge your own feelings as you continue to look into your own eyes. What emotions are going through you right now? How do you feel as you continue to hear your name repeated? Within a few minutes, however, the mirror image begins to blur and

25

fade, and when it clears, you are able to see your face as you've always seen it. The only difference is the gleam in your eyes.

Knowing that it is time to go, you climb into your boat once more, and you pull the warm blankets around you. This time it begins to float in the opposite direction, taking you back from whence you came. You gaze up at the trees, watching the ripples of the breeze fluttering through the leaves, and soon you hear the birdsong once more. Emerging from the tunnel of trees into a place where the sky is clearly visible, you notice that it has become night, and the stars are twinkling brightly overhead. The boat slips into the cave, and soon you begin to feel yourself rising from the soft blankets in the boat. As you rise, you become more and more aware of your surroundings, and soon you are able to sense the furniture beneath you. This is the room from which you began this journey not so very long ago. As you become more and more aware of the room around you, you remember the face in the mirror, an image that will stay with you as you awaken from your rest.

Taking three deep breaths, one for body, one for mind, and one for spirit, you open your eyes to find yourself in a familiar place.

Your Thoughts and Feelings:

Day 5: What Am I Being Asked to Do?

"Whether I shall turn out to be the hero of my own life, or whether that station will be held by anyone else, these pages must show..."

- Charles Dickens, *David Copperfield*

Based on your reflection from yesterday about the face in the mirror and the examination of your feelings, what do you feel it is that you are called to do? How is this pending journey appropriate for the heroic archetype you have selected for yourself?

Fully describe a goal you are working toward. What is the purpose of this goal? What will it help you to achieve after attaining it? What strengths do you possess that will help you along the way?

What am I being asked to do?

_____

_____

_____

_____

_____

_____

_____

_____

_____

Day 6: Regrets Only

Find a comfortable position in a quiet place where you will not be disturbed. Read the meditation slowly and carefully. Be sure to pause to allow for visualization.

Close your eyes and relax. Now take three deep breaths: one for body, one for mind, and one for spirit. Take one last very deep breath and hold it. Just when you think you cannot hold the breath any longer, pull in just a bit more air. Again, when you feel as if you cannot continue holding the breath, pull in just a little more. When you finally do release your breath, do so very slowly in a long continuous exhale until you have released all that you were holding. Breathe slowly and deeply as you continue to relax. Relax all the muscles of your body: your legs, your arms, your shoulders, and your jaw. Completely relax.

Imagine that you are sinking down into the furniture, and in turn sinking through the floor. Allow yourself to continue sinking down and down, all the while feeling completely relaxed. You pass deep down into the earth and suddenly find yourself in a vast cavern, nestled comfortably in the bottom of a shallow boat. This time, however, you notice that the temperature is much cooler than last time. Fortunately, you are wrapped in warm blankets. Pulling them close and snuggling into them, you feel comfortable and very relaxed.

The boat again begins to drift along with the current of the narrow river. A stronger breeze is blowing once you emerge into the open, and the boat begins to rock a bit. The motion lulls you into a deeper state of relaxation, as if you are in the arms of a loving mother who is gently rocking you. Even though it is mid-afternoon, the skies are rather grey, and the air is chilled. You pull the blankets even more closely about you as the boat continues to float along. The familiar tunnel of trees begins to envelope your boat, and you notice that

29

most of the leaves have already fallen. The crisp smell in the air tells you that winter seems to be fast approaching. The wind through the branches carries a mournful sound and the only birdsong today is the cawing of a crow. You see him perched above the boat as you float by, and he seems to be looking at you. How does this make you feel?

Floating along, the boat eventually takes shore on the same sandy bank it had on your previous journey; however, it does not look entirely the same. Even though it is now winter, more than the season has changed since your last visit. The very large, very old tree is gone, and in its place is a rotting stump. Discarded leaves from the surrounding trees swirl like dervishes in the cold wind that blows through the area. How do the changes make you feel? What other differences do you note?

Stepping out of the boat, you are glad to find that there is a warm coat tucked into the prow. You slip it on and pull the collar very tightly to your chin to keep out the cold. As you walk around the old stump, you happen to catch the late daylight reflecting off something that seems to be carelessly tossed inside the hollow. Even though the stump is filled with decaying leaves, something seems to be sticking out from beneath the partial covering. Reaching down, you discover that it is the mirror you left behind after your last visit. Sadly, the mirror's handle has dulled from being exposed to the elements, and the mirror itself is cracked. No sound comes from the mirror this time.

When you hold the mirror up to your face, you see a reflection in the cracked glass. It is the heroic archetype you saw once before, but he/she has aged considerably. Looking even more closely, you notice that the gleam has gone from his/her eyes, and a slight tear trickles down his/her cheek. As much as you would rather look away, you find that you are compelled to look at the face in the mirror. What feelings are going through you at this moment? A drop of water splashes onto the glass of the mirror, and you realize that a tear has fallen from your own eye. Slowly, the splashed tear seems to spread across the glass, and the mirrored image swirls. A faint voice, recognizable as the one from your call to adventure, whispers, "Why? Why did you forsake me?"

Your own voice trembles as you tell the image that you'd never forgotten him/her; it's just that there were reasons for not answering the call. Tell him/her what your reasons were. Was it self-doubt? Was it fear? Did someone else have something to do with it? Be honest with your archetypal hero... he/she is part of you.

While you've been talking, the mirrored image has been swirling. Once you are finished with your explanation, the mirror clears once again, but you notice that the crack has disappeared. Your tears have healed the mirror. Looking inside, you see the hero once again, and even though he/she still looks aged, there seems to be a gleam returning to his/her eyes. Perhaps the call has not been lost forever. Perhaps it's not too late to answer it.

This time when you get into your boat, you take the mirror with you. Taking care to lay it gently among the blankets, you climb in, wrap yourself up, and lie down. As you become comfortable once again, what emotions are going through you now? Be cognizant of your feelings as the boat carries you back to the starting place. After emerging from the tunnel of trees, you notice that once again, it has become night. This time, though, there is a huge, full moon hanging in the sky above you. Its light shines down on you, bathing you in its brilliance. Imagine that you can breathe in the light of the moon. How does it make you feel? How can you change the image in the mirror to become that of the vibrant hero it once was?

The boat slips into the cave, and soon you begin to feel yourself rising from the soft blankets in the boat. As you rise, you become more and more aware of your surroundings, and soon you are able to sense the furniture beneath you. This is the room from which you began this journey not so very long ago. As you become more and more aware of the room around you, you remember the face in the mirror, an image that will stay with you as you awaken from your rest.

Taking three deep breaths, one for body, one for mind, and one for spirit, you open your eyes to find yourself in a familiar place.

Your Thoughts and Feelings:

_____

_____

_____

_____

_____

_____

_____

_____

_____

_____

_____

_____

_____

_____

_____

_____

Day 7: Why Am I Hesitating?

"The mass of men lead lives of quiet desperation."

- Henry David Thoreau, *Walden,* 1854

US Transcendentalist author (1817 - 1862)

Based on your reflections from yesterday about the face in the mirror and the examination of your feelings, what do you feel it is that you could do to alleviate the pain of the inner hero? How might refusing to act on the call have a negative impact on successfully completing your journey? Is there an outside force holding you back?

Re-examine your goal. What fears or weaknesses within you need to be overcome in order to attain this goal? Do not reflect upon outside obstacles. What knowledge or skills do you lack at this point which may hinder your progress if not addressed?

Why am I hesitating?

_____

_____

_____

_____

_____

_____

Day 8: When Presents Present Themselves

Find a comfortable position in a quiet place where you will not be disturbed. Read the meditation slowly and carefully. Be sure to pause to allow for visualization.

Close your eyes and relax. Now take three deep breaths: one for body, one for mind, and one for spirit. Take one last very deep breath and hold it. Just when you think you cannot hold the breath any longer, pull in just a bit more air. Again, when you feel as if you cannot continue holding the breath, pull in just a little more. When you finally do release your breath, do so very slowly in a long continuous exhale until you have released all that you were holding. Breathe slowly and deeply as you continue to relax. Relax all the muscles of your body: your legs, your arms, your shoulders, and your jaw. Completely relax.

Imagine that you are sinking down into the furniture, and in turn sinking through the floor. Allow yourself to continue sinking down and down, all the while feeling completely relaxed. You continue to sink down until you find yourself nestling into a pile of soft cushions in a cavernous room. The ceiling is very high, and you notice that the room is circular. Surprisingly, you find the favorite comforts of your own world furnishing this place, giving it a welcoming, familiar vibration. Move around the room and examine these favorites. What are you most surprised to find there? Is it a favorite chair? Your grandmother's kitchen table? A favorite painting that hangs in your best friend's living room? What items decorate this special place?

Among the articles in the room, you find your mirror which reflects your heroic archetype. You are pleased that you remembered to bring it with you after leaving the forest last time, and you gently look to make sure that the previous crack has indeed healed. Seeing that the mirror is whole, you smile and look at your reflection once more. The hero is looking back, this time with a smile. He/She still appears older than the first time you'd seen him/her, but the sadness has disappeared. How do you feel as the hero smiles at you?

You sense a tingling sensation going through you as if the air were suddenly electrified. It fills you with a sense of urgency to do something, as if you can't manage to just sit still. A staccato drumbeat plays faintly in the distance, but begins to increase in volume as the tingling sensation increases as well. A sound of laughter, joyous and welcoming, comes from the mirror. Looking at it, you see the hero not only smiling broadly, but actually laughing. The sound of the drumbeat increases and the hero calls loudly, "Are you ready?!" A vibration comes through the handle of the mirror, riding up your arm and permeating your entire body. In shock, you drop the mirror, shattering it to pieces. The drum beat increases as the hero seems to rise from the place where the glass had been in the mirror and then stands before you. Still laughing, he/she puts his/her arms about you in a tight hug. The vibrating sense increases as you and the hero merge into one. He/She has always been a part of you, but you are now absolutely aware of that inner presence. How does this make you feel?

Once the merging has taken place, the sound of the drum begins to lessen and fade. The tingling in your body also begins to dissipate, yet the feeling of urgency to do something still remains. After a few moments, you notice that the drum beat had been replaced by the sound of someone knocking on a door. You feel a bit disoriented after your experience, yet the knocking continues. A voice from deep within whispers, "Follow your bliss and doors will open where there were no doors before." What does this mean to you? How does that idea make you feel?

Looking around the room, you suddenly notice that a door has appeared where there had been none previously. You are startled at its sudden appearance, and you hesitate to move toward it, even though the knocking is becoming more insistent. Again, the voice from deep within whispers, "When the student is ready, the teacher will appear." What feelings are going through you now?

Gathering your courage, you move toward the door. As you do so, the knocking stops. As soon as you hesitate, however, the knocking begins again. Trusting your inner voice, you again head toward the door, and the knocking ceases once more. Someone knows you are coming. Who do you suppose is on the other side of that door? Who do you hope it is? Who do you fear it is?

Take a deep breath and grasp the door handle. Opening it boldly, you find the stoop is vacant. In place of a person that you expected to see (because, of course, someone must have been knocking), you find a large, beautifully gift-wrapped package. You look out into the darkness for a glimpse of the person who was knocking, but there is no one there. Picking up the package, you discover that there is a tag on the gift. It has your name on it. Looking about one last time before closing the door, you carry the gift to the center of the room. Setting it down on the floor, you sit cross-legged in front of the package to get a better look at it. Fully describe the package. How is it decorated? Are there any ribbons or bows? What color is the gift-wrap? How do you feel as you sit and gaze at it?

After looking at it for some time, your curiosity gets the better of you, and you decide that it's time to open the gift. Because you sense the importance of the gift, you open it slowly, with purpose. When you finally open the gift, what do you find? What do you think you are supposed to do with it? Is it something you already know how to use, or is it something you will have to learn to utilize? How does this gift make you feel? Who do you suppose sent it?

It will take you some time to think about the importance of the gift, and so you decide to set it in a special place in this room. Where is that special place? The gift will be safe because as you look around you, you notice that the door has disappeared once more, and the room is once again a continuous circle.

Lie back down upon the soft cushions, and think about the events of this visit. Your inner hero still whispers to you. What is he/she saying? While you are listening, you find yourself becoming more and more drowsy. A rest will do you good now that you have decided to follow through with your call. Curling into a comfortable position, you soon you begin to feel yourself rising from the cushions. As you rise, you become more and more aware of your surroundings, and soon you are able to sense the furniture beneath you. This is the room from which you began this journey not so very long ago. As you become more and more aware of the room around you, you remember the gift in your special place, an image that will stay with you as you awaken from your rest.

Taking three deep breaths, one for body, one for mind, and one for spirit, you open your eyes to find yourself in a familiar place.

Your Thoughts and Feelings:

_____

_____

_____

_____

_____

_____

_____

_____

_____

_____

_____

_____

_____

_____

_____

_____

_____

_____

_____

_____

_____

Day 9: What's Kicking Me in the Butt?

"Chance is always powerful. Let your hook be always cast; in the pool where you least expect it, there will be a fish."

-- Ovid

Roman poet (43 BC - 17 AD)

Ask yourself what outside forces drive you toward your goal. What situations seem to pop up that remind you and keep you focused on your goal? How might you feel if you were to ignore the "nudges" you get? If you don't pay attention right away, do the "nudges" keep popping up? What is "kicking you in the butt" to keep you focused?

Think about the gift that you received from your unknown benefactor. What about the gift calls you to action? What do you suppose you are supposed to do with the gifts and talents you have within yourself? Identify at least three gifts you already possess, and explain how you can use each one to help you achieve your goals.

What's kicking me in the butt?

_____

_____

_____

_____

_____

_____

Day 10: Taking Leave

Find a comfortable position in a quiet place where you will not be disturbed. Read the meditation slowly and carefully. Be sure to pause to allow for visualization.

Close your eyes and relax. Now take three deep breaths: one for body, one for mind, and one for spirit. Take one last very deep breath and hold it. Just when you think you cannot hold the breath any longer, pull in just a bit more air. Again, when you feel as if you cannot continue holding the breath, pull in just a little more. When you finally do release your breath, do so very slowly in a long continuous exhale until you have released all that you were holding. Breathe slowly and deeply as you continue to relax. Relax all the muscles of your body: your legs, your arms, your shoulders, and your jaw. Completely relax.

Imagine that you are sinking down into the furniture, and in turn sinking through the floor. Allow yourself to continue sinking down and down, all the while feeling completely relaxed. You continue to sink down until you find yourself nestling into a pile of soft cushions in a cavernous room. The ceiling is very high, and you notice that the room is circular. Painted on the ceiling is an intricate design that resembles a compass. Getting up, you find the favorite comforts of your own world furnishing this place, and feel once again that welcoming, familiar vibration. Turn around very slowly and take a good look at your room. You will find your favorite furniture, and your favorite décor. Breathing deeply in contentment, a familiar delicious scent wafts to your nostrils. Surprised, you look to find that a plate of the food you love most is waiting for you. It is just the right temperature, and there is a beverage alongside it. A small card placed next to the plate says, "To fortify you". Not wanting your favorite food to either get too cold or to melt, you sit at the table and eat heartily. As you fill your stomach, a sense of satisfaction and energy permeate your body. You feel wonderful, as if you could accomplish anything.

After eating, you decide to get a better look at the gift you received on your last visit. You go to get the box so that you can bring it to the table. When you come back, you find that the dirty dishes have disappeared, leaving the table neat and clean. If only the everyday world worked that way!

Open the box and remove what is inside. Take a good look at it under the light. What does it do? What do you suppose it is for? Holding it in your hands, it feels "right" in them. It's true... this is YOUR gift. How do you plan to use it? Looking into the box, you notice a small card that you hadn't seen earlier. It says, "To aid you". Take another good look at your gift. How can this aid you?

While you are looking at the gift, you suddenly hear a knock. Startled, you notice that a door has once again appeared in your room, although it is in a different place this time. There are beautiful intricate designs on the wall around the door that continue up toward the ceiling. Looking up, you notice that the door is directly below a particular direction on the ceiling's compass design. Which direction does the door face? Why do you suppose the door faces this direction? What could it mean?

Next to the door, a coat rack has appeared. Upon the coat rack, you notice that there is a garment hanging. What does it look like? What kind of garment is it? What color is it? Examining it closely, you find a tag attached which says, "To protect you". How can this garment offer protection? From what could it save you?

The knocking has begun again, more insistent than before. The voice deep inside you questions once more, "Are you ready?"

You know now that the only way to achieve your chosen goal and to heal your heroic archetype within is to go through that door. The knocking persists. Your journey awaits.

You have been fortified. The food has left you feeling energetic and strong.

Knocking again. Help awaits you in the form of your gift, even it you do not yet know how to use it.

Still more knocking. You have protection from your garment, and you put it on. It fits perfectly as if it had been made just for you. Rest assured; it has. There is a satchel or backpack hanging beside the garment on the coat rack. You place your gift inside the bag and swing it over your shoulder. Placing your hand on the doorknob, you turn it slowly and open the door. The knocking has stopped, and peering outside, no one is there to greet you. Still, you are not afraid. You know that the journey of a thousand miles begins with the first step. How do you feel as you extend your right foot to begin that journey? What does this journey mean for you? What will it eventually mean for others because you dared to take the journey?

Stepping out onto the stoop, what do you see around you? Fully describe your surroundings. Is there a path or a road? Or must you forge your own? Come down the steps as you begin to walk your chosen path. Where do you hope it will lead? Who do you hope to meet? Who are you afraid to run into? No matter what, you have your garment of protection, and you have your gift. All will be well.

Knowing this, you decide that there is one last thing you must do before embarking into the unknown. The one thing you have yet to do is rest up for the journey. It will be long, and it will not always be easy. You re-enter the room through the door so that you may rest your body for the trials ahead. This time the door does not disappear. You have already crossed its threshold, and you have made your decision to follow through on your quest. All you need now is some last minute rest.

Lying down upon the cushions, you find yourself feeling comfortably relaxed. Soon you begin to feel yourself rising from the soft blankets in your special place. As you rise, you become more and more aware of your surroundings, and soon you are able to sense the furniture beneath you. This is the room from which you began this journey not so very long ago. As you become more and more aware of the room around you, you remember your preparations for your upcoming journey. You are fortified, you will be aided, and you are protected. These images and feelings will stay with you as you awaken from your rest.

Taking three deep breaths, one for body, one for mind, and one for spirit, you open your eyes to find yourself in a familiar place.

Your Thoughts and Feelings:

_____

_____

_____

_____

_____

_____

_____

_____

_____

_____

_____

_____

_____

_____

_____

_____

_____

Day 11: Putting One Foot in Front of the Other

"There are two mistakes one can make along the road to truth...not going all the way, and not starting."

-- Hindu Prince Gautama Siddharta, the founder of Buddhism, 563-483 B.C.

What first steps have you taken in order to become successful in attaining your desired outcome? How are you putting "one foot in front of the other" in order to move forward? Be specific in describing the steps you are taking in order to reach your goal. How have you been "fortified" for the journey? What tools do you have to aid you? What protection do you take with you? Just how prepared are you to move forward?

How am I putting one foot in front of the other?

_____

_____

_____

_____

_____

_____

_____

_____

_____

Day 12: In the Pit

Find a comfortable position in a quiet place where you will not be disturbed. Read the meditation slowly and carefully. Be sure to pause to allow for visualization.

Close your eyes and relax. Now take three deep breaths: one for body, one for mind, and one for spirit. Take one last very deep breath and hold it. Just when you think you cannot hold the breath any longer, pull in just a bit more air. Again, when you feel as if you cannot continue holding the breath, pull in just a little more. When you finally do release your breath, do so very slowly in a long continuous exhale until you have released all that you were holding. Breathe slowly and deeply as you continue to relax. Relax all the muscles of your body: your legs, your arms, your shoulders, and your jaw. Completely relax.

Imagine that you are sinking down into the furniture, and in turn sinking through the floor. Allow yourself to continue sinking down and down, all the while feeling completely relaxed.   You continue to sink down until you find yourself nestling into a pile of soft cushions in a cavernous room. The ceiling is very high, and you notice that the room is circular. Smiling, you remember this place, and you gaze up at the compass markings on the ceiling for a few moments. You really hadn't taken the time to study them earlier, but each direction has intricate symbolic images painted nearby. Examine the images painted to represent each of the four directions. What do you see? What images are specifically painted next to the direction that is above your door? Contemplate on why you have been guided to begin your journey in this particular direction.

Standing up, you still find the favorite comforts of your own world furnishing this place, giving it a welcoming, familiar vibration. Your garment and your satchel containing your gift are ready and waiting for you to recover from your rest. After sleeping for what seems like a few days, you are energized and ready to begin. While heading to the door, your nostrils are once again treated to the scent of your favorite breakfast waiting for you. A small sign next to the plate says again, "To fortify you." Eat heartily, yet savor the flavors for you do not know for sure when your next hot meal will be. What nourishes you?

You put on your garment, and once again you turn back to the table to find that the plates have already been cleared. Looking around, you nod and know that it is finally time to go.

Step up to the door. This is it. This is finally the beginning of your journey that you have been preparing for. The hero within whispers ever so gently, "What are you waiting for?" Smiling, you head out the door to find the sun shining brightly. The door closes behind you, and you step lightly down the stairs. What do you see? What surrounds you? Is there a path, or must you forge one of your own?

The moment your foot reaches the ground, you feel a sudden cold chill in the air, and a sound, like a small avalanche, reaches your ears. Turning around, you are astounded to see that the door is retreating into the distance. The building seems to be being pulled away from you by some invisible force, eventually leaving you in the midst of an empty clearing. The disappearance has left you a bit unsettled because it took with it all your familiar treasures; you truly are alone. What feelings are going through you right now? You know that there is no going back the way you came for the door has vanished. You must delve into the unknown with only your garment of protection and your gift. Do you still feel ready?

You decide that it is probably best for you to follow the direction you'd seen indicated above the door. Taking a deep breath, you look forward to try to find your way. Although it seems to be cluttered with vegetation of some kind, you suddenly notice a very faint path you hadn't seen at first. It looks as if it has not been traveled on in a very long time. This seems to be the best place to start.

Stepping onto the path, you notice that the trees and branches seem to part for you to walk forward easily. You do not find it necessary to grope gingerly to make progress. In fact, it seems so easy that you begin to take quick strides in the hope of finding something, anything up ahead. What do you expect to find? What do you seem to be hurrying toward? Just as soon as you get too comfortable with practically running down a path that seems to open up for you, you realize that you should have been more careful. Your guard has been let down because it has been too easy. Before you can fully comprehend what is happening, two branches part and you rush forward only to find yourself falling into a black hole. The hole is very deep and when you finally hit the bottom, it is fortunate that you are not seriously injured. Standing to test your sore muscles, look around. After examining your plight, you realize that there is no way for you to climb out. The edges are very smooth, and there is nothing for you to grip. How are you feeling now?

You sit on the floor of the pit and think about how easily the journey started. Paths were opening up for you as if by magic only to lead you to this? One thing, though, that you consider, is that you would not have fallen in if you'd have been paying attention. You got caught up in running toward the destination that you really didn't watch out for the path you were on.

Your first lesson: Avoid focusing only on the end product without paying attention to detail along the way.

At the moment, there is nothing you can do to get out. Yelling has produced nothing more than an echo off the smooth walls and a raspy voice, and so you sit silently on the ground. All the running through the trees has made you tired, and you decide to take a rest before figuring out what to do. It's fortunate that you have your garment with you, as it protects you from the chill in the air. Lying down on the ground, you soon feel as if you could sleep for a very long time. Staring up at the opening far above you, you find that the moon is out. Just the sight of the moon comforts you and reminds you of the strength and light you pulled in the last time you gazed up at her from the boat. Breathe deeply and pull in that light once more. All will be well. You will find your way out, but sleep is calling first. One last glimpse of the moon, and you close your eyes.

Lying down on the ground, you soon you begin to feel yourself rising from it. As you rise, you become more and more aware of your surroundings, and soon you are able to sense the furniture beneath you. This is the room from which you began this journey not so very long ago. As you become more and more aware of the room around you, you remember your first lesson, one that will stay with you as you awaken from your rest.

Taking three deep breaths, one for body, one for mind, and one for spirit, you open your eyes to find yourself in a familiar place.

Your Thoughts and Feelings:

_____

_____

_____

_____

_____

_____

_____

_____

_____

_____

_____

_____

_____

_____

_____

_____

_____

_____

Day 13: Facing the Darkness

"The Chinese use two brush strokes to write the word 'crisis.' One brush stroke stands for danger; the other for opportunity. In a crisis, be aware of the danger - but recognize the opportunity."

- Richard Milhous Nixon

Now that you are committed to following through with moving toward your desired goal, how does that make you feel? Sometimes it's a dark and scary feeling to tread in unfamiliar territory. What makes you feel uncomfortable about the journey ahead? What obstacles, as yet unknown to you, MIGHT you have to face? How does that make you feel? How do you feel that no matter what, you are committed to following through? Feel the fear and do it anyway!

What might I have to face?

_____

_____

_____

_____

_____

_____

Day 14: Diligence Pays Off

Find a comfortable position in a quiet place where you will not be disturbed. Read the meditation slowly and carefully. Be sure to pause to allow for visualization.

Close your eyes and relax. Now take three deep breaths: one for body, one for mind, and one for spirit. Take one last very deep breath and hold it. Just when you think you cannot hold the breath any longer, pull in just a bit more air. Again, when you feel as if you cannot continue holding the breath, pull in just a little more. When you finally do release your breath, do so very slowly in a long continuous exhale until you have released all that you were holding. Breathe slowly and deeply as you continue to relax. Relax all the muscles of your body: your legs, your arms, your shoulders, and your jaw. Completely relax.

Imagine that you are sinking down into the furniture, and in turn sinking through the floor. Allow yourself to continue sinking down and down, all the while feeling completely relaxed.   You continue to sink down until you find yourself curled up, awakening at the bottom of the pit into which you'd fallen. Although it is a bit cold and damp, you are not afraid, and the rest has done you good. You are confident that you will find a way to get out of this place and continue your journey.

You stand up and stretch, bending slightly at the waist to the left and to the right. Rolling your head slowly in circles, you work the kinks out of your neck from sleeping on the ground. While you are stretching, rain suddenly begins to fall lightly. Stand still with your arms outstretched and let the rain wash over you. It is refreshing in spite of the fact that you are in the bottom of a deep pit. Let it run into your hair while you run your fingers in a circular pattern in your scalp. Open your mouth wide to accept the refreshment that has been offered to you. So many others might have viewed the rain falling at this time to be something negative, saying, "Great. Just what I need right now!" in a sarcastic tone. Fortunately, you know better... it IS what you need right now. Allow the blessing of the water to fill you.

It's time for you to better assess your situation. Again, you look for handholds so that you might climb up and out, but there are none. Even though the walls are packed dirt, they are very smooth, and the rain has made them slippery. Moving around the circumference of the pit, you very carefully run your hands over the walls trying to find any roots that may be sticking out that you may use as rungs. While you are doing so, your hands come across a depression in the wall that you hadn't noticed before. It's very slight, but enough for you to begin digging with a fingernail. Small clumps of dirt begin to fall away as the depression seems to formulate into a crack in the wall. Eagerly, you begin digging away with your fingers at the crack, and before long, the crack begins to reveal the outline of a doorway. Ignoring the pain in your tortured and bleeding fingers, you continue to pull away the dirt, using some of the rainwater pooled on the ground to help soften and loosen the soil. After a few hours, you find yourself standing in front of a door that had been concealed by a dirt covering. Rejoicing loudly, you push with all your might against the door until it finally begins to move ever so slightly. The adrenalin pumps through you, making you feel stronger than you know you should be after these hours of digging. At last the door opens when you throw your entire weight against it, and you fall through the opening.

You can't believe your luck. A long, dark tunnel proceeds beyond the doorway, and you notice that there are torches already burning brightly to light your way. Going back to gather your garment and your satchel, you enter the tunnel and begin to make your way along it.

The tunnel winds back and forth, to the right and to the left, and soon it is difficult to figure out which direction you are heading. So far, there is only one passageway, so at least you know for sure that you haven't made any wrong turns. Where did this tunnel come from? Who might have built it and why? These questions run through your head as you continue walking along this strange path. Shadows form on the wall, making you feel as if you are not alone. Looking back, all you see is your own shadow in the flickering light.

The further you go into the tunnel, the cooler the air becomes. Fortunately you have your garment to keep you warm. Put it on and keep walking.

After a short time, you begin to hear the sound of falling water. Excited, you begin to mover quicker along the passage, but this time you are more wary of your surroundings. You do not want to fall into another pit! The floor becomes wetter as you continue, and soon the tunnel opens up into a huge cavern. Look up. The ceiling is gleaming from the torchlight reflecting off the beautiful crystals that protrude from the rock. What color are they? What kind of crystals do you suppose they are?

To your left, you see a waterfall coming down from an opening high above, splashing into a beautiful subterranean lake. Thirst overcomes you, and you move to the water's edge to take a drink. After splashing some water to wash your face, you proceed to drink the most delicious, refreshing water you can ever remember. You sit down on a rock nearby to rest and take in your surroundings. What else do you see in this cavern? Describe this place in great detail. Do you see any items laying around that you might want to pick up? Look around to see what you can find. Place anything you wish to take with you into your satchel. What have you found?

Returning again to the water's edge, you notice a large pile of soft moss, about the size of a bed, growing there. After the strain of your earlier digging and the long walk through the tunnel, you realize just how exhausted you are. The moss is so inviting, and when you sit on it, you feel how soft and comfortable it is. It makes a wonderful bed after sleeping the ground last night.

Wrapping yourself up in your garment, lie down and stretch your body. Although it may ache a bit from the hard labor you'd done, you know that this is a good type of ache...one that comes from hard work that produces results. So many others might have resigned themselves to the fate of dying in the pit because they didn't pay close attention to detail. They probably would have given up and wasted away, but not you. You were rewarded for your diligence. Congratulations.

Smiling, you close your eyes, knowing that after you've rested, you will be able to resume your journey. Take a deep breath and feel yourself drifting away into the darkness. Soon you begin to feel yourself rising from the soft moss in this beautiful cavern. As you rise, you become more and more aware of your surroundings, and soon you are able to sense the furniture beneath you. This is the room from which you began this journey not so very long ago. As you become more and more aware of the room around you, you remember how your attention to detail and your hard work paid off. You are proud of yourself and believe that you can overcome any obstacle along your road of trials. These images and feelings will stay with you as you awaken from your rest.

Taking three deep breaths, one for body, one for mind, and one for spirit, you open your eyes to find yourself in a familiar place.

Your Thoughts and Feelings:

_____

_____

_____

_____

_____

_____

_____

_____

_____

_____

_____

_____

_____

_____

_____

_____

_____

_____

_____

Day 15: Ease on Down the Road

"Certainly, travel is more than the seeing of sights; it is a change that goes on, deep and permanent, in the ideas of living."

- Miriam Beard

What outside obstacles must be faced in order to achieve your goal? How will you successfully overcome these obstacles while still maintaining your true sense of self? How can you honestly bring about change without compromising your own principles or values? What can you do to help yourself "ease on down the road"?

How am I easing on down the road?

_____

_____

_____

_____

_____

_____

Day 16: The Mentor Appears

Find a comfortable position in a quiet place where you will not be disturbed. Read the meditation slowly and carefully. Be sure to pause to allow for visualization.

Close your eyes and relax. Now take three deep breaths: one for body, one for mind, and one for spirit. Take one last very deep breath and hold it. Just when you think you cannot hold the breath any longer, pull in just a bit more air. Again, when you feel as if you cannot continue holding the breath, pull in just a little more. When you finally do release your breath, do so very slowly in a long continuous exhale until you have released all that you were holding. Breathe slowly and deeply as you continue to relax. Relax all the muscles of your body: your legs, your arms, your shoulders, and your jaw. Completely relax.

Imagine that you are sinking down into the furniture, and in turn sinking through the floor. Allow yourself to continue sinking down and down, all the while feeling completely relaxed.   You continue to sink down until you find yourself curled up, awakening upon a pile of soft moss. It's very comfortable upon the pile, especially after the physical labor of a few hours before. Your arms feel a bit stiff as you stretch them out before you, and you remember how vigorously you'd been digging out the dirt in the wall to uncover the hidden door. Even though your fingers are aching and horribly scraped up, you feel a sense of accomplishment. These are "battle wounds" that you sustained, and you have come out a survivor. For that, you should feel proud.

Sitting up, you dip your sore hands into the cool water in the lake beside you. It soothes the aching a bit. You splash some of the water on your face to fully refresh you before taking a long drink. The water in your belly reminds you that you haven't eaten in quite some time.   Looking down into the water, you see there the reflection of your inner heroic archetype. He/she is smiling at you, but is also urging you to get up and start moving. "Let's move forward," he/she seems to be saying.

Stand up and look around. The torches are still burning. The light reflected off the crystals that adorn the ceiling and walls dances off the surface of the lake. Ripples created by the falling water make the light shimmer, so that even the cavern walls seem in motion. How do you feel as you continue to watch the light?

Pick up your satchel and examine the items that you'd found in the cave before you fell asleep. What do you have? Unfortunately, none of the items are edible, and so you must go in search of food. Wrapping your garment warmly about you, begin to walk along the lake's edge to see where it takes you. Keep your eyes open for any passages that may veer out of the cavern.

As you walk along, your footsteps make a crunching sound on the gravel of the floor. You are half tempted to wade in the water as you walk, but common sense tells you that it would probably be best to try to remain dry. Still, you are feeling adventurous and light-hearted, wanting to play as you move along. At one point, you even find yourself laughing a bit. What is it that is making you feel so jovial? Many others might feel afraid at being in an underground cavern, not knowing where to find an exit...but you do not. Your optimism truly keeps you moving forward. And so you walk. And you walk. And you continue to walk.

Having kept to the water's edge, you are certain that you could not have taken any wrong turns. What you had originally categorized as a lake seems more like a river at this moment. A current has developed, and the water is moving rather swiftly. How odd that you hadn't noticed it earlier. A good thing about a river, though, is that the water must be moving toward an exit somewhere. The question is, how far away is that exit? Your optimism is starting to fade a bit as it feels as if this cave has no end.

Your stomach is really beginning to growl now. How long has is been since that marvelous breakfast in your room? It feels like days have gone by.

Coming around a bend, you notice that the river branches off into two tributaries, each one eking off into a separate tunnel. One goes off toward the left while the other veers only slightly to the right. It would be easy to remain walking along this bank and continue with the right hand branch, but what if the left branch is the one that will take you where you want to go? Remember, you still have your quest to fulfill. Do you remember what it is? What is the purpose of this journey to begin with? Where are you trying to get to? Feeling a bit of frustration at your indecision, you say aloud, "Which way am I supposed to go?"

Your second lesson: Ask and it shall be given to you.

While you are standing there trying to figure out which leg of the river to follow, you hear a light splashing sound behind you. Thinking that there might be a fish jumping in the water, you look back. You don't see anything at first because you had come from around a bend when you got to this place. But there is that sound again, and again in a rhythmic pattern. A few moments later, you are astonished to see someone punting a raft along the river. Before long, the raft comes alongside the shore right near you. Who is the person steering the raft? What does he/she look like?

Stepping onto the shore, the newcomer drags the raft out of the water so that it will not float away. He/she turns to you with a stern look at first that melts into a genuine grin. You are so astonished that you haven't moved from your spot. He/she greets you with a slap on the shoulder as he/she walks past you to sit down on a large rock. No words as yet have been spoken, but he/she beckons you to sit down as well.

"Come. I have something for you," the mysterious stranger says. He/she reaches into a bag slung across his/her shoulders and from within he/she brings out a loaf of bread and a block of cheese. Using a large knife hanging from an ornate belt, he/she cuts off a large wedge of cheese before tearing off the heel of the bread. Handing them to you, he/she smiles.

Cocking your head to one side, you look sidelong at the stranger, not sure if you should trust him/her or not; however, your hunger gets the best of you. Nodding to the stranger and accepting the food offered, you begin to eat, slowly at first, but with more vigor as your appetite gives in. Remembering your manners at last, you mumble a thanks under a deep blush. You didn't realize just how hungry you were!

No other words are spoken as you both share in this meal although you look curiously at one another. What is going through your mind while you look at him/her? What do you suppose he/she is thinking about you?

Once you have finished eating, you find the courage to ask questions. "Who are you? What is your name?" What is his/her reply?

"How did you come to find me? What are you doing here?" Again, pay attention to the response.

One thing you do learn is that this person is your guide. Reaching into his/her pouch once more, he/she produces a map, which he/she hands to you. It does not look like any map you've ever seen before. For one thing, none of the markings are familiar. There aren't any of the streets or towns that you know from your own world. Your destination has already been marked with a red star; however, it is not labeled with the name of a place. It is labeled with the accomplishment of your goal. In which direction does your destination lie? What does that mean to you?

In order to continue, your guide tells you that you must decide which of the two branches of the river you must take. Will it be the one that goes off to the left, or will you stay on the path that only veers slightly to the right? At least now you have transportation, for your guide has volunteered his/her raft to take you whichever way you want to go. Which do you decide to take? Why this one and not the other?

Stepping onto the raft, you remember that it was only when you asked aloud for guidance that your mentor appeared. Take to heart lesson two.

Your guide points to a soft pile of blankets in the center of the raft and tells you that it is probably best for you to rest right now. You cannot help but agree, and you lie down among the blankets after first making sure that your satchel was securely wedged among them so as not to roll off the raft. Sleep comes to you almost instantly as the rhythmic sound of the punting lulls you. Take a deep breath and feel yourself drifting away into the darkness. Soon you begin to feel yourself rising from the soft blankets upon this raft. As you rise, you become more and more aware of your surroundings, and soon you are able to sense the furniture beneath you. This is the room from which you began this journey not so very long ago. As you become more and more aware of the room around you, you think about how your mentor appeared only after you'd asked for help. The image of his/her face and feelings you had at meeting him/her will stay with you as you awaken from your rest.

Taking three deep breaths, one for body, one for mind, and one for spirit, you open your eyes to find yourself in a familiar place.

Your Thoughts and Feelings:

_____

_____

_____

_____

_____

_____

_____

_____

_____

_____

_____

_____

_____

_____

_____

_____

_____

_____

_____

_____

Day 17: Who or What Has Inspired Me to Keep Moving?

"Teachers open the door. You enter by yourself."

- Chinese Proverb

What mentor/helper do you have on your journey to guide you? What skills/talents do they possess that you would like to acquire within yourself? What tools have you been given that will help you along the way? What strengths do you have available within you?

Who or what has inspired me to keep moving forward?

_____

_____

_____

_____

_____

_____

_____

Day 18: Parley With the Adversary

Find a comfortable position in a quiet place where you will not be disturbed. Read the meditation slowly and carefully. Be sure to pause to allow for visualization.

Close your eyes and relax. Now take three deep breaths: one for body, one for mind, and one for spirit. Take one last very deep breath and hold it. Just when you think you cannot hold the breath any longer, pull in just a bit more air. Again, when you feel as if you cannot continue holding the breath, pull in just a little more. When you finally do release your breath, do so very slowly in a long continuous exhale until you have released all that you were holding. Breathe slowly and deeply as you continue to relax. Relax all the muscles of your body: your legs, your arms, your shoulders, and your jaw. Completely relax.

Imagine that you are sinking down into the furniture, and in turn sinking through the floor. Allow yourself to continue sinking down and down, all the while feeling completely relaxed. You continue to sink down until you find yourself curled up, awakening upon a pile of blankets in the center of a moving raft. Looking up, you find your guide is looking at you, as if to ask if your rest has been adequate. The last thing you remember was getting on the raft after pointing out which direction your guide should take on the underground river.

Up ahead, you see that the river is exiting from the cave. At last! You've been led out of the subterranean dimness! As the raft floats closer to the exit, you feel more and more excited to see the sun once more. The cave becomes brighter and brighter as you approach, and your eyes are having difficulty in adjusting to the light. Squinting, you look ahead to try to catch a glimpse of the world beyond the cave. What are you feeling as you finally leave the darkness?

Look around and take in your new surroundings. The river seems to flow onward. Describe the new setting. Is it a tropical jungle? A forest? A flat plain? Where is this river leading you?

You turn to ask a question of your guide and find that he/she has disappeared. You are left alone on the raft. At first you begin to panic, but then you remember that your guide has given you a map. Pull it out of your bag and look at it. Try to figure out where you are in relation to the red star that marks your goal. How far do you have yet to travel before arriving?

Look around for landmarks. What do you see that can give a clue to your whereabouts as they relate to the map?

While you are looking around, you notice that a loaf of bread and some fruit are lying on the blanket. Your guide has left food for you. Not knowing how long it will be before your next meal, eat only enough to satisfy your hunger and put the rest in your bag.

Look again at your map. In order to get to your destination, will you be staying on the raft and traveling by water? Or will you have to leave the raft to move inland? Wherever you need to go, be sure to follow directions carefully. You do not want to get lost.

Following your chosen course, you move along for several hours. For the most part, they have been uneventful. Describe the landscape through which you are moving. What is the path like? Does the river twist and turn, or is it a straight course? If you are on land, what is the terrain like? Pay attention to specific details no matter what course you are on... the details hold meaning for you. Look at the specific types of plants or trees you may see. What sounds do you hear? Is there any animal life? Birds? All of these things mean something as part of your journey.

Reaching into your satchel, you withdraw a booklet and a pencil which you'd found when exploring the cave. They were part of the items left laying around that you'd picked up. Make a list of all the specific items you see so that you can think about their meaning later.

While you are writing, a slight breeze begins to blow. It feels cool and refreshing against your cheek. Close your eyes and let it play with your hair, tossing it in the breeze. Turn your face upwards toward the sun and allow it to warm you. Suddenly, out of the breeze you hear a soft whisper. It is the sound of your name on the wind. Before this, you'd felt warmed by the breeze, but now there is a chill developing. The sound of your name comes to you again, bringing with it another chilling zephyr.

Looking around, you try to find the origin of the voice. Where does it seem to be coming from? Is it ahead of you, or behind you? Or is it to the right or left of you? Does the sound seem to come from above or below? Try to figure out where the voice is coming from.

When you determine the direction, what do you intend to do? Will you follow the sound? Or will you ignore it and move forward? What feelings are going through you as you make your decision?

Ultimately, because the sound of your name is insistent, you decide to find the origin of the voice. Turn towards the sound and move in that direction. As you step closer and closer, notice that the air becomes colder and colder. The sound becomes louder. At first it seemed like a beckoning, but now it is more of a command. Even so, you decide to continue to move toward it. You have completely abandoned your path in an effort to satisfy your curiosity about finding the owner of that voice. What does it sound like? Describe its pitch and intensity. Does it sound like someone you know? Or is the voice new to you?

Coming around a bend (either on the terrain or on the raft), you see someone off in the distance. Describe what you see. Do you know this person? Who is it? If you do not know the person, who do you suppose it might be? What do you think he/she wants with you?

Come close to the person who has called to you. The air is very cold now as you stand there face to face. How are you feeling? What thoughts are going through your mind as you look quietly at one another?

"Where are you headed?" the person asks. Tell him/her where you are going. "Why do you want to go there? Nothing awaits you in that place! Why not come with me?" What goes through your mind at the offer?

You recognize that this person is an adversary and not a guide. How is it that you know this? What feelings or thoughts bring you to this conclusion? Although you realize his/her adversarial status, you do not feel afraid. He/She merely looks at you quietly. This is not a confrontation, but a sizing up of the one that must be resisted for you to continue. Looking into his/her eyes, what do you see there? The eyes are the window of the soul, and it is often there that you can find a person's true intent. What is it you see in your adversary's eyes? Is it anger? Jealousy? Resentment? What resides there that might make this person attempt to keep you from moving toward your goal?

Once you recognize his/her motivation, it makes it easier to resist. He/She extends his/her hand to you. What do you do? This person wants you to follow his/her path instead of your own. How does that make you feel? He/She smiles at first, continuing to whisper your name. He/She backs slowly away but with hand outstretched toward you. Resist the temptation to go with him/her. Remember, he/she has questioned your journey and has told you that nothing awaits you there.

Breathe deeply and think about your inner hero. Will following this person best honor your inner hero? Although you want to hear advice from that inner voice, nothing comes. You must make the decision yourself, trusting what is right for you.

You put your hands in your pockets because of the chill in the air. When you do, you feel something in your right hand pocket. Taking it out, you notice that it is one of the items you picked up inside the crystal cavern. What is it? What can you use it for? Just seeing this object helps you to find the necessary courage to walk away.

You begin to back away, and your adversary barks out your name. The friendly smile has vanished and is replaced by a hard, cold expression. Feeling your courage rise, stand and face your adversary, looking him/her square in the eye. You will not be tempted, or bullied, or made to feel guilty about following the path that is right for you. Hold tight to the object in your right hand. It seems to fill you with courage. Each person has his/her own path to follow, including your adversary. Maintaining that eye contact, bow your head slightly to show respect for him/her, but let him/her know by your facial expression that you choose to return to your own path.

In frustration, your adversary turns on his/her heel and stalks away in the other direction. You, too, turn to go back toward your path. As you walk away, you hear on the winds, "We shall meet again." What are your feelings as you hear these words?

Even though you keep checking over your shoulder, your adversary is not following. Find your path once more. Is it the river? If so, return to your raft. If you were on the terrain, face the direction of your goal. In either case, take a deep breath and feel a sense of accomplishment in resisting the temptation to leave your chosen path. However, you are emotionally drained and physically tired. Sit for a moment and refresh yourself with the food that you saved from your breakfast.

Confident that you are safe in this place, make a bed for yourself either in the middle of the raft, or along the side of the trail. In either case, you are comfortable and warm. You have your garment of protection that will keep you safe as you sleep. After first stretching full length, curl up into a comfortable position and prepare to nod off. Take a deep breath and feel yourself drifting away into the darkness. Soon you begin to feel yourself rising from the soft blankets. As you rise, you become more and more aware of your surroundings, and soon you are able to sense the furniture beneath you. This is the room from which you began this journey not so very long ago. As you become more and more aware of the room around you, you think about how your adversary and how you'd managed to resist him/her. The image of his/her face and feelings you had at meeting him/her will stay with you as you awaken from your rest.

Taking three deep breaths, one for body, one for mind, and one for spirit, you open your eyes to find yourself in a familiar place.

Your Thoughts and Feelings:

_____

_____

_____

_____

_____

_____

_____

_____

_____

_____

_____

_____

_____

_____

_____

_____

_____

_____

Day 19: Who or What is Holding You Back?

"You can discover what your enemy fears most by observing the means he uses to frighten you."

- Eric Hoffer

     Who or what seems to want to hold you back? How does it make you feel to be pulled in the opposite direction of that which you wish to go? How do you overcome the temptation to turn back in spite of what he/she/it is either promising if you do, or threatening if you do not? How do these outside influences make you feel? How do you feel when you are able to stand up to whatever is holding you back?

Who or what seems to be holding me back?
_____
_____
_____
_____
_____
_____
_____

Day 20: A Friend in Need

Find a comfortable position in a quiet place where you will not be disturbed. Read the meditation slowly and carefully. Be sure to pause to allow for visualization.

Close your eyes and relax. Now take three deep breaths: one for body, one for mind, and one for spirit. Take one last very deep breath and hold it. Just when you think you cannot hold the breath any longer, pull in just a bit more air. Again, when you feel as if you cannot continue holding the breath, pull in just a little more. When you finally do release your breath, do so very slowly in a long continuous exhale until you have released all that you were holding. Breathe slowly and deeply as you continue to relax. Relax all the muscles of your body: your legs, your arms, your shoulders, and your jaw. Completely relax.

Imagine that you are sinking down into the furniture, and in turn sinking through the floor. Allow yourself to continue sinking down and down, all the while feeling completely relaxed.   You continue to sink down until you find yourself awakening after a satisfying rest. You feel refreshed and ready to move forward on your journey.

Opening your satchel, you pour the contents on the ground to take stock of what you have with you. What items do you have in there? How can they be helpful on this journey? You also come across the notebook in which you were listing things that you noticed while floating along on the raft. Look over your list. Each thing on it has some sort of significance to you.

For example, if you noticed a bed of luscious red roses and their scent was alluring to you, then it is possible that the roses symbolize a quest for love. What did you see?   What does each one symbolize? How does that relate to you and to your journey? Make notes in your book.

Pick up the gift you'd received in your special room... the one that had come in the beautifully wrapped package. Examine it closely. What can it be used for? How do you intend to use it on this journey?

After carefully taking stock of your items, put them away in your satchel. Only you will know the proper time and place to make use of them. For now, it is time to move ahead. You get up onto your feet and begin moving along the path. As you walk, you have become used to paying attention to your surroundings. What do you see today? How do you feel as you continue on your way?

By mid-day the road comes to an abrupt halt at the edge of a steep cliff. If you are still on the raft, you see that the river ends in a long, steep waterfall. No matter how you arrived at the edge, be sure that you remain far enough away to avoid going over. The abyss seems to have no bottom, at least from your point of view. It's about fifty feet to the other side. Looking to the left and to the right, you cannot see a bridge anywhere that can take you across. How do you feel as you seem to come to a dead end? What thoughts go through your mind as your forward progress seems thwarted?

Taking the map out of your satchel, you look at it to see if there is a way across the chasm. The narrowest place between the two sides seems to be several miles to the east. However, your destination lies in a north-westerly route, albeit on the other side of the chasm. Perhaps if you went west, you could find a way to get across without going that far out of your way. Then again, the map shows a widening of the chasm in the west. After deliberating for a while, you decide to go with the map and head east.

Picking up your satchel, you follow the cliff moving in an easterly direction. You must be careful of your footing so that you do not fall in. You know that your final destination lies behind you, but you are forced to take this detour. How do you feel about this?

Walking along, you notice a small house off in the distance. A fire is burning because there is smoke coming out of the chimney. You can even smell meat cooking, making your stomach rumble. Moving at a quick pace, you approach the house. Before going up to the door, however, take a quick look around to be sure that it is safe. What does the yard look like? Describe the house itself. How do you feel as you stand there in the yard? Trusting your intuition that everything is ok, walk up the steps to the front door and knock on it. At first there is no reply, but you see the curtains at the window move a slight bit. Someone is inside. Knock again.

A moment later, the door opens, and you are surprised to be greeted by the guide who had taken you along the river. Smiling broadly, he/she motions for you to come inside. Stepping across the threshold, you cannot help but take in the aroma of roasting meat. It smells so good, especially after eating nothing but bread, cheese, and fruit for past few days.

"What brings you here?" your guide asks. Tell him of your adventures, being sure to mention your parley with your adversary. He/she nods as he/she listens, and smiles when you mention that you have been using the map to find your way. Ask him/her about the narrow point on the map between the two sides of the chasm and if there is a way to get across.

"Of course there is a way. But you cannot do it alone."

You are thankful that it seems you shall have company for your journey. It has been a long one so far, and it will be good to have a fellow traveler along. Your host provides you with a large bowl of hearty stew, piping hot from the Dutch oven over the fire. Its aroma is tantalizing, and you desire to dig in as fast as you can. Taking care not to burn yourself, begin feasting on the delicious stew. As you do, feel the strength surging through your body. You feel as if you could conquer anything.

"You will want to set out soon so that you can get across before dark," your mentor says once you have eaten.

"Yes, you are right," you reply. "Let us get going."

"Us? No, I won't be accompanying you."

Now you are confused because you'd thought that he/she would be going with you to help. After all, he/she had said that you couldn't get across the chasm alone. Remind him/her of those words.

"Yes, it's true that you cannot cross alone, but I never said that I was going with you."

"But who?" you ask.

In reply, your guide opens the front door and steps out onto the porch. You follow him/her outdoors and are surprised by what you see.

At the foot of the steps is your best friend in all the world. He/She has come here to help you accomplish your goal. How do you feel as you see your friend standing there? What is it about this person that makes him/her your best friend? What other obstacles have you gone through together?

You greet one another in warm hug, and then turn to your guide to thank him/her for the hospitality. He/She smiles and hands you a sack of food to take along on the journey. You gladly accept the gift and ask if he/she has any parting advice. What is his/her reply?

You and your companion pick up the path that heads east, and before long you notice that the other side of the chasm is now only about twenty five feet across. This is the point where you must cross, but how? Look at your friend and come up with a plan to get to the other side. You must work together in order to complete the task. What ideas do you have? Do you have any items in your bag that might help you? What about your companion's ideas? Does he/she have anything with him/her that could help you?

Fully describe both the plan and the process you use to get across to the other side. Only through cooperation will you be able to complete the task. How will you work together?

After a few hours, your plan is successful. You are both safely on the other side! How did you do it? What tools did you use? How do you feel about having accomplished this task? How do you feel about having your companion with you for this part of your journey?

Once on the other side, you both are exhausted. You agree that you will rest for a few hours before heading west to pick up the proper trail that leads toward your destination. Your companion has agreed to accompany you for a time, and you are grateful for the company.

Stretching out your limbs to work out any kinks, you then curl up in a comfortable position. The night air is cool, but not cold, so it is comfortable for sleeping. An orange quarter moon hangs in the sky overhead, looking down on you and creating a sense of peace in your heart. Take a deep breath and feel yourself drifting away into the darkness. Soon you begin to feel yourself rising from your bed in the outdoors. As you rise, you become more and more aware of your surroundings, and soon you are able to sense the furniture beneath you. This is the room from which you began this journey not so very long ago. As you become more and more aware of the room around you, you think about your best friend and how he/she had come just when you needed him/her most. The image of his/her face and feelings you had about working with him/her will stay with you as you awaken from your rest.

Taking three deep breaths, one for body, one for mind, and one for spirit, you open your eyes to find yourself in a familiar place.

Your Thoughts and Feelings:

_____

_____

_____

_____

_____

_____

_____

_____

_____

_____

_____

_____

_____

_____

_____

_____

_____

_____

Day 21: Who or What Can I Count On?

"Be courteous to all, but intimate with few, and let those few be well tried before you give them your confidence. True friendship is a plant of slow growth, and must undergo and withstand the shocks of adversity before it is entitled to the appellation."

- George Washington

First president of US (1732 - 1799)

Whenever you are in trouble, who is it that you can count on? Of course, your family will be there for you, but what about your friends? Who among them would be willing to support you in all your endeavors? What strengths do you share with your companions? How can you support each other? What weaknesses do you recognize in yourself that your friend can compensate for? How does that make you feel? Make a list of five people outside your family that you could count on in times of trouble.

Who or what can I count on?

_____

_____

_____

_____

_____

Day 22: Haunted Memories

Find a comfortable position in a quiet place where you will not be disturbed. Read the meditation slowly and carefully. Be sure to pause to allow for visualization.

Close your eyes and relax. Now take three deep breaths: one for body, one for mind, and one for spirit. Take one last very deep breath and hold it. Just when you think you cannot hold the breath any longer, pull in just a bit more air. Again, when you feel as if you cannot continue holding the breath, pull in just a little more. When you finally do release your breath, do so very slowly in a long continuous exhale until you have released all that you were holding. Breathe slowly and deeply as you continue to relax. Relax all the muscles of your body: your legs, your arms, your shoulders, and your jaw. Completely relax.

Imagine that you are sinking down into the furniture, and in turn sinking through the floor. Allow yourself to continue sinking down and down, all the while feeling completely relaxed. You continue to sink down until you find yourself awakening after a satisfying rest. You feel refreshed and ready to move forward on your journey. Looking up, you find your best friend has already risen and is preparing breakfast for you. It is fortunate that he/she remembered to pack additional food from the house before leaving since the two of you ate your mentor's gifts the previous evening. Both of you sit and share a meal, comfortable in the silence between you.

After eating, it is time to begin the trek towards the west to get back on your path. The sun warms your back as you begin, and the day promises to be a glorious one. How do you feel as you move on with your friend at your side? What does the countryside look like? Take note of the types of plants, animals or birds that you see... they do hold meaning for you. Keep a list in your notebook to refer to later.

What do you and your friend talk about on the journey? What is his/her goal that he/she is working toward? How can you help? He/She has already helped you in getting across the chasm. What can you do for him/her?

Finally you reach your path. On the other side, you can take a look at where you'd come from earlier. It seems like a long time ago since you'd been standing on the opposite side of the chasm, trying to figure out how to get across. And now here you are. How do you feel?

Taking out your map, you consult with it to make sure that you are going in the right direction. Your friend also takes a map out of his/her pocket. How wonderful that it seems that you will still be traveling in the same direction! Smiling, the two of you face the journey and continue. Describe the path that you are now on. What can you see in the distance? How much further is your destination?

After traveling all day, the sky becomes darker and you decide to camp for the night. You have a rolled up blanket that you'd taken from the raft. Spreading it on the ground, you make a place to rest near the small fire you and your companion have built. What do you two talk about?

At some point in the conversation, you mention the gift you'd received from a mystery person back in your special room. Take it out of your satchel and show it to him/her. How does he/she react? Does he/she know what the gift can be used for? Listen to his/her suggestions. Look again at the object and try to apply your companion's ideas to it.

Your companion also begins to speak of his/her own goals and dreams. Listen intently. What do your goals have in common? How do they differ? Why do you suppose that this person just happened to be the one to arrive to help you in your time of need?

For some reason, as you listen to him/her describe what he/she plans to accomplish, you begin to doubt your own goal. Compared to his/her goal, yours begins to seem inadequate. Why? What makes you feel that you have to compare yourself to others? What feelings go through you as you continue to listen?

Your friend has become very tired and lies down to go to sleep. You, however, are not yet sleepy enough and wish to sit up for a while. Staring into the fire, the dancing of the flames becomes hypnotic, drawing you into a trancelike state. Your friend's aspirations play in your head, making you feel insecure. What has caused you to doubt yourself? What events in your past have led you to feel insecure in comparison to others? Watching the fire, you begin to see shapes taking form. At first you think you are seeing things, but after a few moments, you note that a scene is being played out for you from your memory. Keep staring into the fire. What do you see? It is something from your past...something that happened long ago that now causes you to feel insecure about other people's successes. What is happening? Relive the scene as if it were happening for the very first time. How do you feel? Who is involved? What is taking place? Pinpoint the event that has led to the insecurity that you feel today.

Now that you have recognized the event, take out a piece of paper from your journal and write down everything that happened exactly as you remember it. Do not leave out any details. Write your feelings as well as your memories. Write and write until you get it all out. Once you have captured it all on paper, tear the page from your journal. With all the emotion you can muster, crumple the paper in your fist and hold onto it as tightly as you can. You are about to destroy that memory, and with it, the insecurity you feel. Wad the paper even tighter in your fist, pouring all the insecure feelings into it. Tighten the muscles of your hand, your arm, and the upper portion of your body. Continue tightening all your muscles until your entire body is filled with tension. Let the tension flow through you and into the wadded paper in your hand. Pull the muscles tighter until they are quivering in tension. When you cannot stand the tension any longer, let go. Completely relax every muscle in your body, including the hand that is holding the crumpled paper. Allow the paper fall into the fire and watch it burn. Stare at the flames and see the painful memory go up in smoke. Let it go. It cannot bother you any longer. How do you feel?

Your companion stirs in his/her sleep, but does not awaken. Look at him/her. How do you feel now?

Sleepiness begins to come over you as you continue to sit by the fire. There is a sense of peace that permeates your body after having let go of your insecure feelings. Relax and allow the peaceful feeling to wash over you. Lying down on your blanket, yawn and look up at the sky. What constellation is overhead at this moment? Why might this be significant for you?

Stretch once more before curling into a comfortable position. Take a deep breath and feel yourself drifting away into the darkness. Soon you begin to feel yourself rising from your bed in the outdoors. As you rise, you become more and more aware of your surroundings, and soon you are able to sense the furniture beneath you. This is the room from which you began this journey not so very long ago. As you become more and more aware of the room around you, you think about the memory you released and how good it feels to no longer carry that burden. The peaceful feelings you experience from letting go will stay with you as you awaken from your rest.

Taking three deep breaths, one for body, one for mind, and one for spirit, you open your eyes to find yourself in a familiar place.

Your Thoughts and Feelings:

_____

_____

_____

_____

_____

_____

_____

_____

_____

_____

_____

_____

_____

_____

_____

Day 23: Making Peace with the Past

"Peace is not a relationship of nations. It is a condition of mind brought about by a serenity of soul. Peace is not merely the absence of war. It is also a state of mind. Lasting peace can come only to peaceful people."

- Jawaharlal Nehru

Indian politician (1889 - 1964)

How have past events had a negative impact upon how you see yourself? How might this have an impact upon whether or not you achieve your desired goals? What memories from your past still haunt you today? How do you suppose you might feel if you had the strength to let go? Try the exercise from the meditation to relieve yourself of negative self-talk and describe how you feel afterward.

How have I made peace with my past?

_____

_____

_____

_____

_____

_____

_____

_____

Day 24: Using Your Gifts

Find a comfortable position in a quiet place where you will not be disturbed. Read the meditation slowly and carefully. Be sure to pause to allow for visualization.

Close your eyes and relax. Now take three deep breaths: one for body, one for mind, and one for spirit. Take one last very deep breath and hold it. Just when you think you cannot hold the breath any longer, pull in just a bit more air. Again, when you feel as if you cannot continue holding the breath, pull in just a little more. When you finally do release your breath, do so very slowly in a long continuous exhale until you have released all that you were holding. Breathe slowly and deeply as you continue to relax. Relax all the muscles of your body: your legs, your arms, your shoulders, and your jaw. Completely relax.

Imagine that you are sinking down into the furniture, and in turn sinking through the floor. Allow yourself to continue sinking down and down, all the while feeling completely relaxed.   You continue to sink down until you find yourself awakening after a satisfying rest. You feel refreshed and ready to move forward on your journey.   The fire has died down and become a pile of smoldering ash, yet still offering warmth in the chill of the morning. Sitting up, you see that you are alone. Your companion has moved on to complete his/her own journey, but has left you a note on your satchel. Pick it up and read it. What does the note say? How do you feel about being left to continue alone?

You also discover that your friend has left some food for you inside your satchel. Take the time to eat before moving forward. As you swallow, feel the nutrients feeding your body, preparing you for the last portion of your quest.

According to your map, you are very near your destination. How do you feel about that? Think about your goal that you have been striving to reach. Describe how you plan to finally attain it now that you are so close. Take inventory of the items in your satchel. What things have you not had the opportunity to use yet? How do you plan to make use of them? What do you suppose they are for? Carefully return them to your bag and prepare to leave. Be sure to scoop dirt over the embers to make sure that they do not ignite and cause an uncontrollable fire. Look around to be sure that you have not forgotten anything.

Taking a deep breath, face the direction you must move in. Where is the sun in relation to where you are facing? How does that make you feel? Allow the sun to shine down on you, bathing you in its warmth before embarking. Close your eyes and feel the warmth penetrate your skin, energizing you and giving you the strength to move on. Take one last breath and extend your right foot. Begin that last long walk toward your goal. This is what you've been working toward. What feelings go through you now?

Start walking. Along the way, be sure to pay attention to any animals, birds, or specific plants you notice. They hold meaning for you and you will remember to contemplate on them later. How significant is it that they happen to cross your path at this time?

You can see your destination in the distance. Your heart begins to race in excitement, but there's also a feeling of tension running through you. What might you feel tense about? Stop and look ahead, feeling the blood pumping through your body as your adrenalin increases. What is it that you see? Fully describe the scene in as much detail as possible. Also, describe anything that you are feeling, whether it is physical feelings or emotional. Prepare yourself to enter the realm of your dreams.

Begin moving forward once more. Starting out slowly and tentatively at first, but your momentum picks up and your pace increases. Your heart is pounding because now you are finally so close after coming so far. Think about all you have experienced on your journey. Remember your gift, the pit, the door, the cave, the river, the mentor, the adversary, the journey, the house, your friend, crossing the abyss, and the fire. Everything you have gone through has been in preparation for this moment. How does that make you feel? How do you believe each step has prepared you for what is to come? What is it you expect to face?

As you are moving along, you suddenly find that your path is blocked. Trying to find a way around the block, you discover that the only way to continue is to somehow get through the blockade. What is it that is blocking your path? What tools might you have to deal with this? Look in your satchel and see what you have in your inventory. Aha! You discover something that is just what you need to remove the blockade. Describe what it is you have. How are you using it? What does it do to remove the block in your path? What happens to whatever is in your way? What feelings go through you as you see your path become visible once more?

You have passed the first test.

Move beyond the block and continue along on your path. How does the temperature of the air seem around you? What do you notice as you go along? Pay attention to as much detail as you can and remember it all for later.

Your destination is much closer now. You can hear sounds on the breeze coming from the place you are heading toward. What do you hear? How do these sounds make you feel? What might be making them? You become even more excited to move quickly onward now and you pick up your pace once again.

All of a sudden you find yourself in some sort of a trap. What kind of trap is it? How have you been captured? Fortunately, you are not injured, but you become frustrated at being stopped once more. Examine the trap carefully... it is not without an escape; however, it is up to you to figure out how to free yourself. Again, search your satchel that is still on your back for anything that might help you solve the puzzle of getting free. What do you have in there that can be of aid? Ah! You discover just what you need... and you had no idea what you have used it for when you'd picked it up in the cave! Work through the secret of the trap until you are able to release yourself. How did you do it?

What have you learned about yourself after making it through the second test?

By this time you are beginning to become impatient to reach the inner realm. It has been so long, and you have been through so much. Keep moving forward. What do you see at this point? Has anything changed about the scenery? What about any sounds that you hear? You stop and being listening intently. Something has caught your attention, even though it is very subtle.

A whisper comes on a chilled wind. "I told you we'd meet again!" The chill moves down your spine as you recognize the voice of your adversary. Even though a moment of fear runs through you, you have come too far to allow anyone to stop you now. That thought gives you the courage that you will need to face your foe.

"I told you that there was nothing here for you. Why didn't you believe me?" Your adversary appears before you after stepping out from behind a tree. Describe what he/she looks like at this moment. How do you feel as you come face to face with the one who wishes to stop you from entering the place you've worked so hard to get to?

Look your adversary in the eye. Take stock of everything you notice about him/her. As you look in his/her eye, you are able to see into his/her soul. For just a few brief moments you are able to see his/her reason for trying to stop you, but astonishingly enough, their reason has nothing to do with you. It is his/her own fears and insecurities that have been projected onto you that makes him/her wish to keep you back. Keep looking into his/her eyes to learn the secret of his/her soul. What do you see there?

He/She realizes what you are doing and breaks eye contact with a loud, angry curse. He/She knows that you have seen his/her weakness. How does that make you feel? What is your attitude about this person now that you know the truth?

Your attitude only angers your adversary even more, and he/she lashes out at you. Ducking behind a nearby tree, you frantically reach into your satchel to find something that can help. When you pull out your hand from the bag, you realize that you are holding the gift that had been given to you at the beginning of the journey. Now is the time to use it. How? How does it work? What does it do? How does it help you to overcome your adversary? Fully describe the battle that wages between the two of you.

You emerge as the victor. What has become of your adversary? Describe what has happened to him/her. How does this make you feel? How do you feel about your victory?

Triumphant, yet exhausted after your ordeal, you must rest before entering the realm of your destination. You have wounds to attend to, whether they are physical or emotional. Take care of yourself first. After coming this far, you must rest before entering.

Lie down upon a patch of soft grass nearby. Its scent is sweet and intoxicating, making you more and more sleepy as you breathe deeply. Look up at the sky to see the stars. There are several constellations overhead; which ones can you see? Why are these significant to you?

Stretch once more before curling into a comfortable position. Take a deep breath and feel yourself drifting away into the darkness. Soon you begin to feel yourself rising from your bed in the outdoors. As you rise, you become more and more aware of your surroundings, and soon you are able to sense the furniture beneath you. This is the room from which you began this journey not so very long ago. As you become more and more aware of the room around you, you think about the tests you have passed. The feelings of pride from this experience will stay with you as you awaken from your rest.

Taking three deep breaths, one for body, one for mind, and one for spirit, you open your eyes to find yourself in a familiar place.

Your Thoughts and Feelings:

_____

_____

_____

_____

_____

_____

_____

_____

_____

_____

_____

_____

_____

_____

_____

Day 25: *Face to Face*

"The meeting of two personalities is like the contact of two chemical substances: if there is any reaction, both are transformed."

- Carl Jung

Swiss psychologist (1875 - 1961)

Who or what is it you must face before you will be able to complete your quest? What fears must you conquer within yourself so that you may be successful? What tests might you have to pass before being deemed worthy to go to the next level? How have your challenges prepared you to face this final test? Be as specific as possible so that when you eventually DO face your adversary, you will be prepared.

Face to Face:

_____

_____

_____

_____

_____

_____

Day 26: The Reward for a Job Well Done

Find a comfortable position in a quiet place where you will not be disturbed. Read the meditation slowly and carefully. Be sure to pause to allow for visualization.

Close your eyes and relax. Now take three deep breaths: one for body, one for mind, and one for spirit. Take one last very deep breath and hold it. Just when you think you cannot hold the breath any longer, pull in just a bit more air. Again, when you feel as if you cannot continue holding the breath, pull in just a little more. When you finally do release your breath, do so very slowly in a long continuous exhale until you have released all that you were holding. Breathe slowly and deeply as you continue to relax. Relax all the muscles of your body: your legs, your arms, your shoulders, and your jaw. Completely relax.

Imagine that you are sinking down into the furniture, and in turn sinking through the floor. Allow yourself to continue sinking down and down, all the while feeling completely relaxed. You continue to sink down until you find yourself awakening after a satisfying rest.

Stretching and looking around, you find yourself just at the gate of your final destination. You've passed three tests to get to this place: the first for clearing what blocks your progress, the second for solving a puzzle to free yourself, and the third for facing your adversary. How do you feel after passing these tests? Reflect once again on how you managed to complete the tasks, and take with you the lessons you learned about how to overcome obstacles.

When you stand up, you notice a pool of clear water nearby. Go to refresh yourself in the pool with a long drink. As you scoop the water in your hands, you can see your reflection in the surface. What you are able to see is your inner hero. Remember which archetype you selected for yourself? Ask

94

yourself how you have honored this archetype on your journey. What accomplishments have you reached that meet the goals of this particular archetype? Spend a few moments looking into his/her eyes in the reflection. What does he/she look like at this moment? Describe the expression on his/her face.

After the long journey, you decide to bathe in this pool of crystal clear water. Disrobe and enter the pool. You are surprised to discover how comfortable the temperature of the water is. Swim about as you bathe, cleansing yourself of the weariness of your travels. Amidst the splashing sounds, you also hear the sound of your inner hero talking to you. What is he/she saying? Listen attentively to what you hear. How do the words make you feel?

Climbing out of the pool, stretch out in the sun to dry. The sun's rays warm your skin, and your complexion is glowing after your bath. This is the cleanest you've felt since leaving the special room so long ago.

Reaching for your garment, you notice that there is something different about it. After the long days on the road, it had been beginning to look a bit shabby and worn. Now, after passing your tests and cleansing yourself, it has transformed. What does it look like now? What do you suppose caused it to change? Put it on. How does it feel against your skin? Look once more at your reflection in the water. What seems different about your appearance?

On either side of the gate there are fruit trees. What kind of fruit do you find growing there? Why might this be significant? Pick some of the fruit for your breakfast and eat your fill. You are almost ready to enter the gate.

Gather your belongings. Your satchel of items seems lighter somehow, even though it still contains the same things. Look again at your special gift and remember how it had aided you in defeating your adversary. How does that make you feel?

Approach the gate, for it is time to enter the realm of your dreams. This is the goal you have been working toward. How does it feel to finally be at the doorstep of achieving it? As you come closer, the door opens of its own accord.

Cross into the place that is key to your dreams. What does it look like? What do you see there? Take the time to fully describe what you see and what you are feeling about being here.

While you are looking around, you hear a slight cough off to your right. Turning to see who is there, you are startled to find your guide waiting for you. He/She smiles and comes forth in greeting. How do you feel about seeing him/her? What does he/she say to you?

He/She begins to guide you along a path that takes you further into the realm of your goals. Describe what you see. At one point, he/she leads you toward a very large table, highly polished and laden with gifts for the completion of your journey. In the center of the table, though, is a raised pedestal. On this pedestal is something very special; it is your reward for a job well done. What is this Ultimate Boon awarded to you? Describe it in detail. What is it? What can you use it for? How can it help you in future journeys? What are your feelings as you hold the treasure in your hand? Remember, you have earned it.

Your guide turns to hug you as you accept your gift, and over his/her shoulder, you catch a glimpse of your reflection in a mirror on the wall behind him/her. Your heroic archetype is looking back at you. Describe his/her reaction to your Boon. How does the achievement of this goal honor your inner archetype?

Turning back to the table, you discover that friends and family have arrived to celebrate your success. Who do you find there? How do you feel at seeing them? What role do these people play in your life? Celebrate with them and begin to connect on a different level now that you've completed this quest. How have you changed? What might this change mean in your relationship with these people? How do you feel about that change?

You spend the rest of the day and evening in celebration. In what ways do you celebrate your victory?

After a long, happy day, your family and friends leave to return home. You know that soon you, too, must return. For now, though, you are still basking in the glory of your accomplishment. Stepping outside, look up at the sky. A full moon is shining once more, bathing you in its light. Allow the energy of the moon to fill you in preparation for the return journey ahead. It, too, will have its perils, but you are more prepared. And you also have your Boon to carry with you.

Re-enter the room where you will be spending the night. A large, soft bed awaits you. It's been a long time since you actually slept in a bed. Stretch out in all directions on the bed and feel the luxury of a mattress beneath you. The pillows are fluffy and soft, cradling your head as you rest it upon them. Pull the warm blankets over you and breathe in the sweet scent of clean sheets. Nestle into a comfortable position and feel sleep begin to overtake you. Take a deep breath and feel yourself drifting away into the darkness. Soon you begin to feel yourself rising from your bed in the outdoors. As you rise, you become more and more aware of your surroundings, and soon you are able to sense the furniture beneath you. This is the room from which you began this journey not so very long ago. As you become more and more aware of the room around you, you think about the tests you have passed and the reward you received for doing so. The feelings of pride from this experience will stay with you as you awaken from your rest.

Taking three deep breaths, one for body, one for mind, and one for spirit, you open your eyes to find yourself in a familiar place.

Your Thoughts and Feelings:

_____

_____

_____

_____

_____

_____

_____

_____

_____

_____

_____

_____

_____

_____

_____

_____

_____

_____

Day 27: What Am I Gaining?

"There is only one success - to be able to spend your life in your own way."

- Christopher Morley

US author & journalist (1890 - 1957)

"Dream Big"

by Emily Shakleton

When I was a little girl

I swore that I would change the world when I grew up

Nothing else would be enough

I see it everyday

We settled for safe

And lose ourselves along the way

`Cause if you don`t dream big,

What`s the use in dreaming?

If you don`t have faith,

There`s nothing worth believing.

It takes one hope

To make the stars worth reaching for.

So reach out for something more!

It took a well perfected plan

For me to finally understand

That it`s not me

Faith is something you can`t see

I wiped my tears away
Now it's time for a change
No I can't waste another day

`Cause if you don't dream big,
What's the use in dreaming?
If you don't have faith
There's nothing worth believing.
It takes one hope
To make the stars worth reaching for.

How have you "dreamed big"? Once you have obtained your present goal, what will you do with your new knowledge/skill/gift? How do you suppose your life will be different once you have succeeded at this task? How may it benefit your life? How might it benefit the lives of others? Remember, we are not heroes for our own glorification, but heroes for what wisdom/gifts/talents we may bring to and share with the world.

What am I gaining?

Day 28: Hesitations

Find a comfortable position in a quiet place where you will not be disturbed. Read the meditation slowly and carefully. Be sure to pause to allow for visualization.

Close your eyes and relax. Now take three deep breaths: one for body, one for mind, and one for spirit. Take one last very deep breath and hold it. Just when you think you cannot hold the breath any longer, pull in just a bit more air. Again, when you feel as if you cannot continue holding the breath, pull in just a little more. When you finally do release your breath, do so very slowly in a long continuous exhale until you have released all that you were holding. Breathe slowly and deeply as you continue to relax. Relax all the muscles of your body: your legs, your arms, your shoulders, and your jaw. Completely relax.

Imagine that you are sinking down into the furniture, and in turn sinking through the floor. Allow yourself to continue sinking down and down, all the while feeling completely relaxed. You continue to sink down until you find yourself awakening after a satisfying rest.

You are so comfortable in the wonderfully soft bed that you almost don't wish to get up. Stretching cat-like, wallow in the luxuriousness of the pillows and the warmth of the blankets. The stress of having to move forward has alleviated, and you begin to feel a bit lazy after having traveled so far. How do you feel as you wake up without the sensation of urgency? Look around the room. Describe what you see in great detail. How does being here make you feel? Looking toward a small table nearby, you notice that a tray has been placed for you. A highly polished silver lid makes you curious to lift it to see the breakfast that awaits you. Step out of bed and lift the cover from the dish. What has been prepared for you? Breathe in deeply, appreciating the tantalizing aroma that makes your mouth water. You are surprised that you are even hungry at all after the feasting of the previous evening, but a familiar rumble begins once the scent reaches your nostrils. Sit down in the well-padded chair and partake of your breakfast with gusto.

While you are eating, your eye falls upon your wonderful reward that you earned for the completion of your task. Bask once again in the feelings of success. What goes through your mind as you look at your reward? How do you plan to use it?

Another thought creeps into your mind, causing you to pause in contemplation. What if you had not been successful in this journey? How might you feel if you had not been able to do what you had set out to? How might things have turned out differently if you'd failed at this attempt? Thinking about this possibility, you walk towards your reward and hold it in your hand. What if this could not have been yours? Would you feel differently about yourself? How do you suppose others might have viewed your failure?

Shaking the thoughts off, you turn once more to your breakfast and clear your plate. Your stomach and your pallet are now satisfied, and so you begin to stretch once more. This place just feels so comfortable right now, and you wish you could stay here. One thing you know, though, is that this is not your home. While it has been a challenge to finally arrive, the quest is now complete. You've done what you'd set out to do, and there is no reason to stay. Actually, now that you have accomplished this task, you feel a sense of urgency to return home to share the experience with others.

Whom do you intend to tell about your adventures? What do you hope will come from sharing what you've learned? Who can benefit the most?

Even though you know that you must get ready to leave, it just feels so comfortable here. The food is delicious, the service is great, and the bed is luxurious. It's hard to leave knowing that you have a long journey back.

Turning toward the bed as if to crawl back in to take a nap, you notice that the bed has mysteriously been made and your cleaned garment is laid out for you in preparation for travel. As much as you'd love to get back into the bed and just relax, you realize that it is important for you to move on. People are waiting for you back home.

Before leaving, you decide that a hot shower is just what you need to get you motivated. Turn the water in the shower as hot as you can comfortably stand it, and step beneath the pulsating stream. Pick up the soap and drink in its fragrance. What does it smell like? Why might the scent be significant for your return journey? What does it remind you of? Allow the hot water to pour over your head. Close your eyes and feel it pulsating against your skull. The sensation is hypnotic and even though your muscles become more relaxed, your spirit becomes more energized for the upcoming journey. Stand there and let the water just come down over your head. Breathe deeply and know that you are ready to share what you've learned. Feel yourself drifting away into the darkness behind your closed eyelids. Begin to feel yourself slowly rising from the shower. As you rise, you become more and more aware of your surroundings, and soon you are able to sense the furniture beneath you. This is the room from which you began this journey not so very long ago. As you become more and more aware of the room around you, you think about the message that you know you must share with others. The feelings stemming from knowing that you have a gift to share will stay with you as you awaken from your rest.

Taking three deep breaths, one for body, one for mind, and one for spirit, you open your eyes to find yourself in a familiar place.

Your Thoughts and Feelings:

_____

_____

_____

_____

_____

_____

_____

_____

_____

_____

_____

_____

_____

_____

_____

_____

Day 29: What If I Haven't Been Successful?

"Don't be discouraged by a failure. It can be a positive experience. Failure is, in a sense, the highway to success, inasmuch as every discovery of what is false leads us to seek earnestly after what is true, and every fresh experience points out some form of error which we shall afterwards carefully avoid. "

- John Keats

English lyric poet (1795 - 1821)

Imagine that you have NOT been able to attain your chosen goal. How might this affect your overall journey? What adjustments might need to be made in the event that the original goal set is unobtainable? Will the possibility of falling short change the way you view yourself, or the way you believe others will perceive you? Do you believe that the effort put into the journey will have been wasted? Or do you believe that learning from mistakes/failure is part of the learning process? Explain your answer in depth.

What if I haven't been successful?

_____

_____

_____

_____

_____

_____

Day 30: Homeward Bound

Find a comfortable position in a quiet place where you will not be disturbed. Read the meditation slowly and carefully. Be sure to pause to allow for visualization.

Close your eyes and relax. Now take three deep breaths: one for body, one for mind, and one for spirit. Take one last very deep breath and hold it. Just when you think you cannot hold the breath any longer, pull in just a bit more air. Again, when you feel as if you cannot continue holding the breath, pull in just a little more. When you finally do release your breath, do so very slowly in a long continuous exhale until you have released all that you were holding. Breathe slowly and deeply as you continue to relax. Relax all the muscles of your body: your legs, your arms, your shoulders, and your jaw. Completely relax.

Imagine that you are sinking down into the furniture, and in turn sinking through the floor. Allow yourself to continue sinking down and down, all the while feeling completely relaxed. You continue to sink down until you find yourself relaxing with a stream of hot water running over your head. The shower is still running, and all the muscles of your body are completely warm and loose. Although the body is relaxed, the spirit is energized for the journey home.

Step out of the shower and wrap yourself in a warm, fluffy towel. Enjoy the feeling of cleanliness in preparation for the return. The pain of all your struggles is washed away, even though you know the journey home will have its own challenges. Helpful things that you have now you'd lacked earlier are your newly gained experience and knowledge, as well as your Ultimate Boon. While you dress in your freshly laundered clothes, in particular your garment of protection, think about how much different you are than when you first began the journey so long ago. What have you learned? How have you changed? How can these changes be helpful in your return trip? Be prepared to be tested at some point along the way. How can your boon help you?

Look at yourself full length in a mirror. At first, you see yourself as you appear to the rest of the world, but upon closer examination, you notice something more. Your reflection has looked like your inner archetype for so long, that you don't see the subtle changes at first glance. How have you changed physically? Look carefully at your entire body and note specific differences. In particular, spend quite a bit of time looking at your face. There is something new in your expression and in your eyes. What is it? Describe the changes. How do you feel about this? Take the time to look yourself square in the eye. Do you like what you see? Why or why not?

After going through the self-evaluation, it is time to prepare to leave. Pack up your satchel, being sure to include your Ultimate Boon. Take a deep breath and look around once more before departing. How do you feel?

Once you are ready to go, you turn to find your mentor is waiting by the door. What advice does he/she give? What seems to be his/her feelings regarding the upcoming journey? He/she informs you that he/she will not be traveling with you, but if needed, he/she will come to your aid. How does that make you feel?

After walking you to the door and leading you to your path, your guide disappears. Face the appropriate direction. Which way are you headed? What is significant about this? Take a deep breath and breathe in the scent of the air. What smells linger? What does the smell remind you of? How does that make you feel?

Begin the trek homeward. As you walk, pay attention to the countryside. What do you see? How is that significant? Describe what you hear as well. Is that the song of a lark or the caw of a crow you hear? How might that be significant?

What is the weather like? Is there any wind? If so, is it a gentle breeze, or a strong gust? What about any precipitation? If there is any, what is happening? How is this important? What does it mean for your journey?

The first three days are uneventful, other than paying attention to your surroundings. You have been keeping a log of interesting things you have noted as you've progressed. Once you return home, you will revisit all your notes to look for significant patterns. Nights have found you sleeping out of doors, but you've been protected. There is food in your satchel so that you have not experienced severe hunger. Everything has been moving along well as you head toward home.

On the fourth day, however, an unexpected challenge arises and may hinder your homeward progress. What is it? What stands in your way now? What tools or knowledge do you possess to help you? How does this obstacle make you feel?

Using everything in your power to overcome this obstacle, you still struggle. Unfortunately, with the struggle comes the return of self-doubt. For a brief time, you begin to doubt that you accomplished anything at all, and that the entire process was a waste of time. How are you feeling at this moment?

The frustration of not being able to solve the problem has made you grow weary. Perhaps if you rest for a bit, a solution to the problem will present itself. Create a bed of leaves for yourself, and take the blanket from your satchel. Sleep has always been good for the mind, the body, and the soul. In the morning, perhaps an answer will arrive. For now, it is time to let it go and try to rest your brain.

Stretch before curling into a comfortable position, then take a deep breath, feeling yourself drifting away into the darkness. Soon you begin to feel yourself rising from your bed in the outdoors. As you rise, you become more and more aware of your surroundings, and soon you are able to sense the furniture beneath you. This is the room from which you began this journey not so very long ago. As you become more and more aware of the room around you, you think about the test that faces you. If you allow it to happen, the solution of the test will somehow come to you as you awaken from your rest.

Taking three deep breaths, one for body, one for mind, and one for spirit, you open your eyes to find yourself in a familiar place.

Your Thoughts and Feelings:

Day 31: What's Getting in My Way?

"Nothing in the world can take the place of Persistence. Talent will not; nothing is more common than unsuccessful men with talent. Genius will not; unrewarded genius is almost a proverb. Education will not; the world is full of educated derelicts. Persistence and determination alone are omnipotent. The slogan 'Press On' has solved and always will solve the problems of the human race."

- Calvin Coolidge

30th president of US (1872 - 1933)

How many times have you achieved something only to run into some outside force that attempts to dampen that accomplishment? Why is it that we sometimes allow things to get in our way just as we reach the brink of total success? The reward has been earned, but what comes next? Sometimes that's the difficult part. While graduation may bring a sense of completion and achievement in earning that diploma or degree, often the graduate wonders, "Now what? What am I supposed to do with this?" With the completion of a stage comes change, and change can be difficult. Often we create our own obstacles to success once we've gotten just so far because of the fear of what comes next.

What things get in your way? Which are external forces? Which internal conflicts must you face? How can you overcome them?

What is getting in my way?
_____
_____
_____
_____
_____

Day 32: Gentle Nudges

Find a comfortable position in a quiet place where you will not be disturbed. Read the meditation slowly and carefully. Be sure to pause to allow for visualization.

Close your eyes and relax. Now take three deep breaths: one for body, one for mind, and one for spirit. Take one last very deep breath and hold it. Just when you think you cannot hold the breath any longer, pull in just a bit more air. Again, when you feel as if you cannot continue holding the breath, pull in just a little more. When you finally do release your breath, do so very slowly in a long continuous exhale until you have released all that you were holding. Breathe slowly and deeply as you continue to relax. Relax all the muscles of your body: your legs, your arms, your shoulders, and your jaw. Completely relax.

Imagine that you are sinking down into the furniture, and in turn sinking through the floor. Allow yourself to continue sinking down and down, all the while feeling completely relaxed. You continue to sink down until you find yourself awakening after an unsatisfying rest.

Having tossed and turned in an effort to come up with a solution to the challenge, you find that you are even more confounded than ever once you awaken to see what is waiting for you. What ever had been placed to challenge you has multiplied in your sleep, and has become even more difficult to overcome. This is what happens when we delay trying to find a solution to our problems; they continue to grow until we either deal with them, or they overwhelm us entirely, and we give up.

Your challenge is now looming over you, and you begin to feel more insecure than ever. "Why did I have to go through all the rest of it only to be stopped now?" you wonder. Look again in your bag and take inventory. Is there anything that you can use? What about any knowledge you have gained? How can that help you now?

Dumping everything from your satchel onto the ground, you begin to sift through aimlessly, barely paying attention to what you are doing. At the moment you are too distracted by your self-doubt to even think clearly. What is going through your mind? What does this situation remind you of? How many times have you completed a task only to feel a sense of not knowing what to do next? What feelings are going through you as you think about these other situations? How did you overcome them in the past? Or did you? Did you give up in the past after having come just so far, only to learn that things had changed and become more difficult? How does that make you feel?

Take stock of your present situation once more. It seems to be growing with each passing moment, and it looks as if you might never return home. For just a moment you begin to believe that maybe it's better that way. If you don't follow through, then not much will be expected from you. Life could be so much easier that way. Sitting on the ground with your back against a tree, you feel discouraged and want to just go back to the place of the luxurious bed and hot shower. That was so much better, and so much easier!

As you sit under the tree, something falls and hits you on the head. Pick it up. How strange—one would expect a nut to fall from a tree, but not this. What is it? Where did it come from? Looking up, try to see where the object has fallen from. What do you see in the tree?

A breeze begins to blow through its branches. At first the only sound is the rustling of the leaves and the swaying of the boughs. After a few moments, the sound of your name seems to be coming on the wind. Gently it comes, gradually increasing in volume and clarity until you are able to recognize the voice of your mentor. He/She begins to speak to you in a soothing and encouraging tone. Once you know who is speaking, listen to what he/she has to say to you. What is he/she saying? What advice is he/she giving you about your self-doubt? Listen carefully, for he/she knows you well.

Suddenly, the breeze turns to a hasty gust and knocks you off your feet. This is your mentor's way of telling you that you need to stop doubting your own abilities and rethink your situation. By using your creativity, you will find an answer to your problem and move forward.

Looking again at your obstacle, it doesn't seem to be a large as it had a short time ago. Did it truly get smaller, or had you been over exaggerating its difficulty? You feel less intimidated now, and decide to once again go through your items to see what can be used. The more you examine them with your new-found boost of confidence, the more ways you begin to see how the items can work together to create what you need to succeed. One of them is your Ultimate Boon and another is the gift you'd received from your mentor so long ago at the beginning of the journey. How do they work together? How does their use help to solve your problem?

Suddenly, without warning, a solution pops into your head. You see in your items a way to use them that hadn't occurred to you earlier. Now that you see it, you realize that the solution is so simple. If you hadn't been so caught up in self-doubt, you would have been able to see it before. Quickly assemble the items to make what you need to remove whatever is blocking your path...success!

A breeze begins to blow once more, and on it you can hear your mentor congratulating you. How does this make you feel?

Once you pass the obstacle, you notice a tunnel up ahead and know that you must enter it in order to return home. Collect your belongings and place them back in your satchel. They have served you well, and you shall treasure them all the more now. Before entering the tunnel, stop alongside a small brook to wash your face and refresh yourself. The water is cool and clear, and you can see your reflection in it, albeit a bit distorted from the current. Even in the moving water you are able to notice a difference in your appearance once again. What is it? How have you changed this time? How does this change make you feel?

Bushes of raspberries and strawberries grow along the brook, and you pause long enough to make a meal for yourself. Small brown trout swim in the brook, and you easily catch a couple to complete your supper. The tiny fire that you've built to roast the fish crackles merrily and makes you feel happy to be on your way once more. Once you've eaten, be sure to carefully douse the fire with water from the brook before leaving.

Now that you have refreshed yourself, you are ready to enter the tunnel that seems to lead into a large cave. Stepping forward, you move along the tunnel, and magically, torches along the sides begin to light your way. This is all very familiar to you, and you soon find yourself within the large crystal cavern you'd entered at the earlier part of your journey. You are certain that this is the way home. However, you are tired from the day's work, and feel the need to rest before continuing. Finding a pile of wonderful soft moss, make a bed for yourself. Tonight's rest will be much more satisfying now that you have overcome your self-doubt and conquered your test.

Smiling to yourself, lie down and look up at the ceiling. What color are these crystals? Why might this be significant? The twinkling of the light reflecting off the crystals has a hypnotic effect, and you soon begin to become very drowsy.

Curl into a comfortable position, and take a deep breath. Feel yourself drifting away into the darkness. Soon you begin to feel yourself rising from your bed of moss in the crystal cavern. As you rise, you become more and more aware of your surroundings, and soon you are able to sense the furniture beneath you. This is the room from which you began this journey not so very long ago. As you become more and more aware of the room around you, you think about how you were able to overcome self-doubt with the help of your mentor. Remember his/her advice, and let the words ring on your memory as you awaken from your rest.

Taking three deep breaths, one for body, one for mind, and one for spirit, you open your eyes to find yourself in a familiar place.

Your Thoughts and Feelings:

_____

_____

_____

_____

_____

_____

_____

_____

_____

_____

_____

_____

_____

_____

_____

_____

_____

Day 33: Who Comes to Your Rescue?

"I was always looking outside myself for strength and confidence but it comes from within. It is there all the time."

- Anna Freud

Austrian psychoanalyst & psychologist (1895 - 1982)

How many times have you completed something only to begin doubting yourself when you actually have to do something with what you've learned? Who is it that comes to your emotional rescue and encourages you to find the strength within yourself to go forward? Who is it that can help you to overcome self-doubt, not through solving your problem for you, but through reminding you of the skills and talents you already possess? How can you continue to come to your own emotional rescue in the future even though you know that this person you trust is only a call away?

Who comes to your emotional rescue?

_____

_____

_____

_____

_____

_____

Day 34: Coming Home

Find a comfortable position in a quiet place where you will not be disturbed. Read the meditation slowly and carefully. Be sure to pause to allow for visualization.

Close your eyes and relax. Now take three deep breaths: one for body, one for mind, and one for spirit. Take one last very deep breath and hold it. Just when you think you cannot hold the breath any longer, pull in just a bit more air. Again, when you feel as if you cannot continue holding the breath, pull in just a little more. When you finally do release your breath, do so very slowly in a long continuous exhale until you have released all that you were holding. Breathe slowly and deeply as you continue to relax. Relax all the muscles of your body: your legs, your arms, your shoulders, and your jaw. Completely relax.

Imagine that you are sinking down into the furniture, and in turn sinking through the floor. Allow yourself to continue sinking down and down, all the while feeling completely relaxed. You continue to sink down until you find yourself awakening after a satisfying rest. Stretch and look upwards. The crystals are twinkling a morning hello and it fills you with cheer, for you realize that you are almost home. Anticipation fills you because you are anxious to share what you have experienced and learned in your absence. Who in particular are you anxious to see again? With whom is it you most wish to share your experiences? Pondering the changes that have taken place in you, how do you imagine that you will be received by this person? By others? How does this make you feel?

Rise from your soft bed of moss and stretch your limbs as far as you can. You search for the source of the sound that acted as a lullaby for you the previous night and soon discover that the gentle waterfall spilling into the underground lake is not far off. Smiling, you remember this place as where you'd found many of the treasures that have helped you in your journey. You remember wondering how these items happened to be lying in an underground cavern and now the answer comes to you. They were purposely left by a previous traveler for the next person to find. Not knowing who the former traveler was, you offer a few words of thanks to this benefactor. It is certain that he/she did not know who would discover the gifts, but he/she made the choice to be of assistance to the next one to find him/her self in the cavern. How does it make you feel to realize that someone left these tools with no thought of reward or thanks, but just the inclination to aid another?

Open your satchel and remove any contents that you believe could be of use to another in the future. Arrange them thoughtfully and resist the urge to leave a note. Leave them for someone else to use just as you did. How do you feel knowing that you are providing for future travelers? How does it make you feel to do this anonymously, without the possibility of any reward or thanks for your actions?

The only things you take with you are your initial gift, your notebook, and your boon. Your load has been lightened tremendously, and the feelings in your heart reflect that. You are truly ready to leave this place. However, you are not quite sure of how to get out. You decide to cleanse yourself in the spray of the waterfall before tackling the business of finding an exit. The sound of the water falling is soothing and you long to feel it splash over your head.

Enter the water and swim toward the falls. Surprisingly, it is a very refreshing temperature and not the chill you initially expected. Play for a bit in the water as you approach the falls. How do you feel at this moment? Tread water for a moment and look around you. What do you see? Describe the place in detail, remembering so that you may write it down when you emerge from your bath.

Coming closer to the falls, dive down below the surface and come up with the water cascading over you. There is a large rock just beneath the surface for you to stand upon so that you may experience the full benefits of the falling water. Let it pulsate against your scalp, invigorating you. It soothingly pelts against the skin to massage out any remnants of weariness from the return journey. You can feel your circulation moving freely through your body, creating new vigor and energy for this last portion of the return. Diving off the rock and into the pooled water, swim around for a few more minutes. Look up at the wonderful waterfall. How do you feel?

As you are looking at it, you notice something you hadn't seen before. At first you cannot believe your eyes, but looking again, you are certain that it is not a mirage. On the right-hand side of the waterfall, there appears to be a formation of crystals that looks like a ladder. Swimming over to the edge, you look up and discover that the ladder leads to where the waterfall emerges into the cavern. You quickly dress and retrieve the items you are taking with you. Gather your initial gift, your boon, and your notebook. Although you must swim back to get to the foot of the ladder, you do not mind so long as you remember to keep your satchel dry by holding it above the water.

Look up. How high must you climb? What is going though your mind as you gaze upwards? How do you feel about climbing the crystal stair? Begin your ascent, being sure to gauge your footing along the way. The crystals form secure hand and footholds in the wall of the cavern, so there is no fear of them dislodging. How do you feel as you are climbing? Are you strong enough to gaze behind you as you proceed? Or might the height frighten you into being frozen to the spot, unable to move? Decide whether you wish to look behind you at this point or not. If you do look back, what do you see from this vantage point? How does it make you feel?

The opening from which the water emerges is only a few more feet away. Climb carefully and bring yourself atop the ledge. The water comes from a large creek pouring into a small opening in the side of a hill. You can see daylight at the end of the short tunnel, and you quickly scramble along the edge of the creek to avoid being caught in the current and pulled over the falls. Emerge into the sunlight, feeling its warmth on your face upon your exit from the cavern.

Looking around, you are surprised to discover where you are. Just across the creek is the place from which you exited at the beginning of the journey. This is the place that had mysteriously disappeared as soon as you crossed the threshold, but here it is, waiting for your return. How do you feel as you see this familiar place?

Quickly crossing the creek, hurry to the door and enter your special place. You are home. Once inside, you see that everything is as you had left it. The one thing you had missed the most was your comfortable bed. Lie down upon it, thankful to be home. Gaze up at the ceiling to see the familiar compass painted there, and smile in the familiarity of home. As you lie there, you begin to drift off into the most comfortable sleep you've had since leaving, even more comfortable than the luxurious bed you'd slept in after your celebration. Nothing can compare to the comfort of home.

Curl into a comfortable position, and take a deep breath. Feel yourself drifting away into the darkness. Soon you begin to feel yourself rising from your very own bed in your special place. As you rise, you become more and more aware of your surroundings, and soon you are able to sense the furniture beneath you. This is the room from which you began this journey not so very long ago. As you become more and more aware of the room around you, you think about how wonderful it is to have such a place as home to return to. This feeling of satisfaction for the completion of a long journey will remain in your memory as you awaken from your rest.

Taking three deep breaths, one for body, one for mind, and one for spirit, you open your eyes to find yourself in a familiar place.

Your Thoughts and Feelings:

_____

_____

_____

_____

_____

_____

_____

_____

_____

_____

_____

_____

_____

_____

_____

_____

_____

_____

Day 35: "There's No Place Like Home"

"A man travels the world over in search of what he needs and returns home to find it."

- George Moore

After having been gone from home for a period of time, how do you feel when returning once more to your home? What do you particularly miss whenever you go away from home? What are you specifically thankful for upon your return? Based on the experiences you have outside your home and away from family, what lessons do you learn that you wish to share with family members? What knowledge do you possess that you can bring home? How can sharing the experiences of our days help to create a more satisfying home life? What do you wish to share with your family and friends?

Your Reaction:

_____

_____

_____

_____

_____

_____

_____

Day 36: Some Will, Some Won't

Find a comfortable position in a quiet place where you will not be disturbed. Read the meditation slowly and carefully. Be sure to pause to allow for visualization.

Close your eyes and relax. Now take three deep breaths: one for body, one for mind, and one for spirit. Take one last very deep breath and hold it. Just when you think you cannot hold the breath any longer, pull in just a bit more air. Again, when you feel as if you cannot continue holding the breath, pull in just a little more. When you finally do release your breath, do so very slowly in a long continuous exhale until you have released all that you were holding. Breathe slowly and deeply as you continue to relax. Relax all the muscles of your body: your legs, your arms, your shoulders, and your jaw. Completely relax.

Imagine that you are sinking down into the furniture, and in turn sinking through the floor. Allow yourself to continue sinking down and down, all the while feeling completely relaxed. You pass deep down into the earth and suddenly find yourself awakening in your bed in your very special place. Stretch cat-line in contentment as you look around your room. Admire your favorite possessions and embrace the familiarity of being home. It almost seems as if the long journey was a dream, and yet you know it was not. Get out of bed and go to each of your special items and remind yourself of why it holds this status for you. Who or what does each remind you of? How does the memory of each make you feel?

Everything is so familiar, and yet you can sense of difference in the air. The difference is not with the place; it is within you. How have you changed? Do these changes make you think or feel differently about being home? How does this make you feel? You realize that your return has left you with an

124

obligation to share what you have learned with others. How do you feel about that?

While you are perusing the room, a pleasant, tantalizing scent wafts in the air. You are suddenly greeted with, "Well, I'm glad to see you're finally back!"

Turning around, you find the one person with whom you wanted to share your experiences sitting at the table. A hearty breakfast awaits you, and the table has been set for two. Who is this person? Why is he/she the one you with which you most wish to share your tale? How do you feel upon seeing him/her? What has he/she prepared for your breakfast in honor of your return?

Greet this person with a big hug before sitting down at the table. The two of you enjoy the wonderful food, and he/she listens to the tales of your adventures. How does he/she react? What does he/she say about what you've learned?

"You've changed," he/she observes. As you continue to talk, it is apparent that he/she approves of the changes in you. How does this make you feel? What does he/she remark about the changes?

As you continue with your meal, it is obvious that he/she is becoming more and more wistful with the description of each adventure. For a moment, you think that he/she is no longer listening and has begun daydreaming. Question him/her about it. How does this reaction make you feel?

His/her response surprises you. He/she tells you that he/she had been contemplating trying something new, but was unsure of whether or not to proceed. However, after hearing your tale, you have awakened in him/her the courage to take that step forward. How does this make you feel? What is it that he/she would like to do? How has your story impacted him/her? What can you do to help him/her get started? You can feel a change taking place in your relationship to this person. What is it? How do you feel about this change?

After finishing breakfast, you talk for a bit more before he/she arises to leave. He/she has many plans to make, and is eager to get started after listening to you. How do you feel about that? He/she gives you a big hug and says that he/she will return soon to talk with you more. Say good-bye and open the door for him/her. When you do, you discover that there is someone else on the doorstep that was just about to knock. Who is this person?

Say good-bye to one friend as you welcome your newcomer. This new person is also a good friend, and you are glad to see him/her. This person, however, does not seem to be as pleased to see you. When he/she enters, he/she barely returns your welcoming hug before taking a seat and turning to you with, "So. You're back." The tone carries something negative, but you can't quite put your finger on what is wrong. You've been so close in the past and are puzzled by his/her reaction.

"So what did you do while you were off on your vacation?" he/she demands. Again, the tone sounds condescending and puts you on your guard. What feelings are going through you? Why might he/she be acting this way?

Try to remain pleasant with this person who obviously isn't. Cheerfully describe your adventures just as you had earlier. Somehow, though, based on his/her stiff reaction, you begin to feel as if you'd done something wrong by going on the journey at all. Where is this feeling of guilt coming from? Why do you even feel guilty at all? You've done nothing wrong, although this person obviously believes you have. What do you suppose has led him/her to the conclusion that your journey was a bad thing? How does that make you feel?

As you talk, you hear yourself downplaying certain parts of the adventure. Why would you censor yourself? Which parts do you downplay? Why? How does it make you feel to know that you cannot share your entire experience with this person because it obviously makes him/her upset? What has caused this chasm in your once-close relationship? How do you begin to feel about yourself as you hear how you downplay your experiences?

His/her comments are repetitive, and all he/she seems to say is, "Oh. Uh huh. How nice for you." How does this make you feel? Why do you suppose he/she is acting like this?

Before long, the conversation becomes too unbearable for you to stand. It seems that the only way to talk to this person is to change the subject entirely and try to talk about something you have in common. However, resentment has begun to build in you, and you find your end of the conversation as stiff as his/hers. How do you feel about this change between you two? Is there anything that can make things be the way they used to be when you were close? How do you see the relationship evolving?

As the conversation becomes more uncomfortable, your companion decides that it's time to leave. At this point you are filled with conflicting emotions. This is someone that you care about, and yet his/her reaction to your journey has left you filled with negative emotions. What are these emotions?

After he/she leaves, the negativity still hangs in the air. While you know that you've done nothing wrong in following your call to adventure, your friend's reaction has left you feeling as if you should not have gone. Ask yourself once again if there is something that can be done to heal the relationship.

You decide that the events of the day have left you tired and confused. You were so happy to share with your first visitor who actually seemed inspired to begin his/her own journey. Revisit those feelings that reinforce the positive aspects of sharing your experiences. Knowing that there is nothing you can do at the moment to change the way your second visitor views your journey, keep your focus on the positive. In your heart, you know that change involves the risk of displeasing those who do not invite change into their own lives. The change in you has changed the relationship, and the change in the relationship is uncomfortable to the person who wished to maintain the status quo. Perhaps, with time, he/she will come to accept what has changed in you and the relationship can grow. If not, are you willing to bear his/her resentment at seeking personal growth?

For the remainder of the day, pour over the extensive notes you took while on your journey. What observations do you make? Pay attention to the types of plants and trees and animals you mentioned in your journal. How were these significant at that point in the journey? Fortunately, you own a book of symbolism. It is a rather large volume that sits high upon one of your bookshelves. Bring it down and begin to look up the significance of everything you wrote in your journal. Even though you have returned, these symbols have lessons to teach you. This is an activity that will bring you much pleasure in the future as you begin to analyze your journey and its significance to your personal growth.

The activity calms your mind and alleviates the negativity you'd felt earlier. You know in your heart that this journey was the best thing for your growth and that no one has the right to negate that growth, no matter who he/she is. Feeling better, you tidy your place after your visits and prepare a simple supper for yourself. Now how do you feel about being home?

Relaxed and calm once more, you decide that it is time to go to sleep. Curl into a comfortable position, and take a deep breath. Feel yourself drifting away into the darkness. Soon you begin to feel yourself rising from your very own bed in your special place. As you rise, you become more and more aware of your surroundings, and soon you are able to sense the furniture beneath you. This is the room from which you began this journey not so very long ago. As you become more and more aware of the room around you, you think about your two friends. Send them both positive thoughts and energy and know that your journey was right for your personal growth. This realization will remain in your memory as you awaken from your rest.

Taking three deep breaths, one for body, one for mind, and one for spirit, you open your eyes to find yourself in a familiar place.

Your Thoughts and Feelings:

_____

_____

_____

_____

_____

_____

_____

_____

_____

_____

_____

_____

_____

_____

_____

_____

_____

Day 37: Staying True to Myself

"Change has a considerable psychological impact on the human mind. To the fearful it is threatening because it means that things may get worse. To the hopeful it is encouraging because things may get better. To the confident it is inspiring because the challenge exists to make things better."

- King Whitney, Jr.

President, Personnel Laboratory Inc.

Think of a time when you shared a new experience with a friend or family member. What was his/her reaction? How do you feel when someone listens to your stories with enthusiasm? How might you feel if that person gained the courage to go ahead and try something new based on what he/she learned from listening to you?

How does it feel when someone dismisses or tears down things that you share? How do you react to his/her negativity? How does that make you feel about what you'd accomplished or about yourself in general? Have you ever had to end a relationship because it could not survive the changes taking place? How did that make you feel?

What changes in your life have been easy? Which have been difficult? Explain.

How will I stay true to myself?

_____

_____

_____

_____

_____

_____

_____

_____

_____

_____

_____

_____

_____

_____

_____

_____

_____

_____

Day 38: A Garden of Memories

Find a comfortable position in a quiet place where you will not be disturbed. Read the meditation slowly and carefully. Be sure to pause to allow for visualization.

Close your eyes and relax. Now take three deep breaths: one for body, one for mind, and one for spirit. Take one last very deep breath and hold it. Just when you think you cannot hold the breath any longer, pull in just a bit more air. Again, when you feel as if you cannot continue holding the breath, pull in just a little more. When you finally do release your breath, do so very slowly in a long continuous exhale until you have released all that you were holding. Breathe slowly and deeply as you continue to relax. Relax all the muscles of your body: your legs, your arms, your shoulders, and your jaw. Completely relax.

Imagine that you are sinking down into the furniture, and in turn sinking through the floor. Allow yourself to continue sinking down and down, all the while feeling completely relaxed. You pass deep down into the earth and suddenly find yourself in a cavern, nestled comfortably in the bottom of a shallow boat. There are soft blankets around you, keeping you warm and relaxed. The boat is caught by the current of a narrow river, and you find yourself floating along, emerging from the darkness of the cave. The river flows through a lush green forest, and the sky above is a deep blue. You are able to lie back, looking up at the trees as the boat continues to float through the forest. As you float along, the tree branches overhead become more intertwined, and the boat enters what seems to be a tunnel through the trees. Even though the sun is now only filtering through the trees, you still feel relaxed and centered as the boat continues on its course. The sound of birdsong lulls you into a deeper state of relaxation, and you watch the gentle breeze rippling the leaves above you.

After a while, the boat gently comes to a stop at a sandy bank. You are now deep in the forest, and the birdsong has begun to dissipate. The only sound at the moment is the gentle rustling of the breeze.

Sit up and look around. You have returned to the place where you first found the mirror and saw the face of your inner heroic archetype. How does it feel to be back here? Step out of the boat. There is sand mixed with the soft grass on the bank, and it is pleasurable to stand there in your bare feet. Explore the small glade in which you find yourself. One thing you are particularly pleased to see is a very large, very old tree. The last time you were here, the tree had been destroyed, but here it is, fully restored. Look around. Everything is in bloom, and the leaves and grasses are greener than you ever remember them. How do you feel being here?

In particular, several plants or flowers catch your eye. Many of those that stand out for you are those that you'd noted while on your journey. What are they? What significance might these particular plants hold for you? Instead of merely writing down which plants you see today, gather a couple of each to take with you. Near the tree you find a small trowel and some potting containers. Carefully dig up each plant or flower, being mindful of the roots. Place each one into its own container and add a bit of earth to protect the delicate roots. Each of these will be replanted into your own little garden just outside the door of your special place as a reminder of your journey. What will each plant or flower remind you of? How does that demonstrate some particular significance from your journey?

Once you have potted all the plants and flowers that you intend to take with you, gently place them in the stern of the boat. It begins to look like a floating garden, and the mixture of colors and scents is pleasing. Put the trowel back next to the tree for the next time you visit. While you are doing that, a slight breeze carries the sound of your name. Smiling, you recognize the voice as that of your inner heroic archetype. Stand up with your arms extended fully, and allow the breeze to blow over you. Your name sounds like music in the air, allowing you to feel as if this is your personal spot in the forest that no one else can experience in the same way. The zephyr is like an embrace. How does that make you feel? What thoughts do you have about being in this place? You know now that you can return here any time you wish, for it has claimed a part of you. Any time you wish to contemplate life's journey, or work out a problem, or simply just to be still, you can get into your boat and come back.

Looking around one last time, turn and head for the boat. It looks beautiful with all the flowers and plants in it. Just as you begin to walk towards your boat, a glint of light off to the right of your peripheral vision catches your attention. It is coming from the hole in the tree. Again, you hear your name on the breeze. Go to the tree to see what it is. Reaching in, you find that something has been left for you. When you pull it out, you discover that your special mirror has been restored. Look into it. Your inner archetype is smiling back at you. He/she is thanking you for honoring him/her with your journey. What else does he/she say to you? What words of wisdom are you left with? How do you feel as you look into his/her eyes once more?

As you continue to look at the reflection, the image begins to swirl and morph into the reflection that you know best. The changes that took place on the journey have become a permanent part of you and are evident in your appearance. Gaze at the image that you present to the world. How does this make you feel?

The completion of this journey has left you with many possibilities for the future. Where is it you wish to go next? What are your plans for future excursions? What do you intend to do with what you've learned from this journey just ended? How can you encourage others to follow their own paths? These are questions that will stay with you as you move on to the next stage of your life. How do you feel about that?

Take the mirror with you as you enter the boat. Anytime you wish to remember that part of yourself, you have no further than your own reflection to turn to. Climb into your boat once more, and pull the warm blankets around you. Take a long look at your garden that you intend to transplant near the door of your special place. Its beauty makes you smile before lying down for the ride back. Snuggle comfortably beneath the blankets and settle yourself.

This time the boat begins to float in the opposite direction, taking you back from whence you came. Gaze up at the trees, watching the ripples of the breeze fluttering through the leaves. Soon you hear the birdsong once more. Emerging from the tunnel of trees into a place where the sky is clearly visible, you notice that it has become night, and the stars are twinkling brightly overhead. While you are looking up, a shooting star streaks across the sky. Make a wish. What is it you wish for? Keep looking toward the sky until it disappears from view as the boat slips into the cave once more. Imagine how you plan to arrange your garden with your beautiful, fragrant treasures. Take in a deep breath and drink in their fragrance once more as you begin to feel yourself rising from the soft blankets in the boat. You know that you can go to your special room any time you wish as well. Your journal and your book of symbolism will always be available for you to return to whenever you want to read through them. You will be able to take your books to sit with them next to your blooming garden and remember the lessons of your journey.

As you continue to rise, you become more and more aware of your surroundings, and soon you are able to sense the furniture beneath you. This is the room from which you began this journey not so very long ago. As you become more and more aware of the room around you, you remember the face in the mirror, your beautiful flowers, and your special places in your imagination. These images will stay with you as you awaken from your rest.

Taking three deep breaths, one for body, one for mind, and one for spirit, you open your eyes to find yourself in a familiar place.

Your Thoughts and Feelings:

_____

_____

_____

_____

_____

_____

_____

_____

_____

_____

_____

_____

_____

_____

_____

_____

_____

Day 39: What Have I Learned?

"Self-reliance is the only road to true freedom, and being one's own person is its ultimate reward. "

- Patricia Sampson

What do you intend to do now that you've completed this journey? What has this particular journey prepared you for? How do you plan to make use of what you've learned and experienced in order to begin your next adventure? In what ways to you feel a sense of freedom to move forward? Has examining the quest of the archetypal hero been a positive or a negative experience for you? Explain in full detail. How might you get more out of your next excursion?

What have I learned?

_____

_____

_____

_____

_____

_____

Day 40: What's Next?

Now that you have completed your Sequential Sojourn, think about the lessons you have learned. In particular, cite three specific things you have learned about yourself that you hadn't realized previously.

You have come full circle, and the new journey begins. What do you imagine your next call will be? Where might it take you? What lessons do you suppose you will have to learn?

We began this journey by examining the heroic archetypes within while reflecting on the words that "a hero lies in you". How has this been proven true in your Sequential Sojourn? How can you keep moving forward?

One thing to keep in mind is that the journey is never completely over. One path merely leads us to the next path on our personal course, and we must find our own way. It is not for us to merely follow the paths of others, but to forge new ones in untrodden territory.

"The Call"
by Susan R. Woodward

Heart pounding;
Thoughts racing;
Breaths deep and full;
A stirring in my breast is nearly a delicious pain--
Urgency.

What I've learned about myself:

_____

_____

_____

_____

_____

_____

_____

_____

_____

No matter where you go in life, remember that it is the journey, and not the destination, that is important!

Acknowledgments

I would like to extend a sincere thank you to Carol Pearson for her kind permission to discuss the twelve heroic archetypes from her book, *Awakening the Heroes Within: Twelve Archetypes to Help Us Find Ourselves and Transform Our World.*

Works Cited

Campbell, Joseph. *The Hero With a Thousand Faces*. New York: MJF Books, 1949.

Carey, Mariah and Walter Afansieff. "Hero". *Music Box*. New York: Columbia Records, 1993.

Pearson, C.S. *Awakening the Heroes Within: Twelve Archetypes to Help Us Find Ourselves and Transform Our World*. CA: HarperSanFrancisco, 1991.

Shackleton, Emily. "Dream Big". Los Angeles: 19 Entertainment, 2008.

Simmons, Gene, Paul Stanley, Lou Reed, and Bob Ezrin. "A World Without Heroes". *Music from "The Elder"*. New York: Ace in the Hole Studios, 1981.

www.ingramcontent.com/pod-product-compliance
Lightning Source LLC
Chambersburg PA
CBHW080050280326
41934CB00014B/3272